All the Best

Songs for Kids

230 Praise Songs, Choruses, and Children's Favorites for Preschool Through Preteen

Compiled by Ken Bible

Songbook Edition

Lillenas PUBLISHING COMPANY

KANSAS CITY, MO 64141

CONTENTS

1

Clap Your Hands

Adapted from Psalm 47:1 by G. J.

GARY JOHNSON

2

If You're Happy

Traditional
Arr. by Lyndell Leatherman

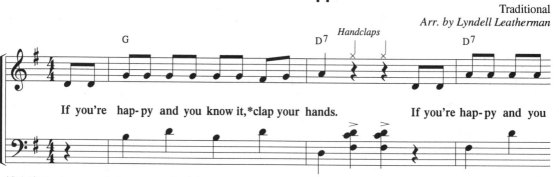

*Substitute: stamp your feet, say amen, do all three.

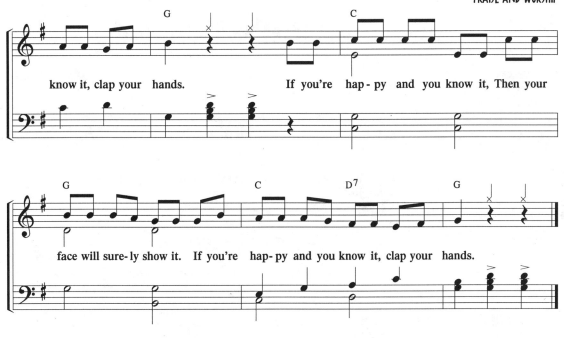

know it, clap your hands. If you're hap-py and you know it, Then your

face will sure-ly show it. If you're hap-py and you know it, clap your hands.

Let's All Sing Together

3

JOY RAMON

Pennsylvania Folk Song
Arr. by Joy Ramon

Let's all *sing to-geth - er; You sing, I sing.

Let's all sing to-geth - er; Sing, sing, sing.

*Substitute: clap, tap, jump, march. "Sing," "clap," and "march" verses on recording.

4 Jesus, We Just Want to Thank You

GLORIA GAITHER and
WILLIAM J. GAITHER

WILLIAM J. GAITHER

*1. Je - sus, we just want to thank You.___
2. Je - sus, we just want to praise You.___
*3. Je - sus, we know You are com - ing.___

Je - sus, we just want to thank___ You.
Je - sus, we just want to praise___ You.
Je - sus, we know You are com - ing.

Je - sus, we just want to thank You,___
Je - sus, we just want to praise You,___
Je - sus, we know You are com - ing;___

Thank You for be - ing so good.___
Praise You for be - ing so good.___
Take us to live in Your home.___

*Verses 1 and 3 on recording.

Praise Him, Praise Him

Anonymous

1. Praise Him, praise Him, All you lit - tle chil - dren;
2. Love Him, praise Him, All you lit - tle chil - dren;
3. Thank Him, thank Him, All you lit - tle chil - dren;

God is love, God is love.
God is love, God is love.
God is love, God is love.

Praise Him, praise Him, All you lit - tle chil - dren;
Love Him, love Him, All you lit - tle chil - dren;
Thank Him, love thank Him, All you lit - tle chil - dren;

God is love, God is love.
God is love, God is love.
God is love, God is love.

6 Sing Alleluia

Words and Music by
GARY JOHNSON

Sing al-le-lu-ia, sing al-le-lu-ia, Sing al-le-lu-ia to the Lord.____ Sing al-le-lu-ia, sing al-le-lu-ia, Sing al-le-lu-ia to the Lord.

7 Sh-h-h-h

Words and Music by
MARIE H. FROST

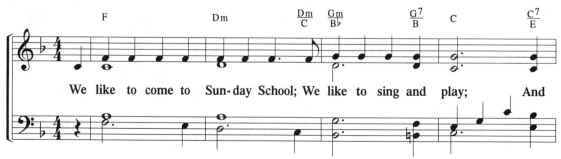

We like to come to Sun-day School; We like to sing and play; And

when it's time to talk to God, We fold our hands and pray. Sh-h-h-h *(spoken)*

It's Good to Give Thanks

8

Adapted from Scripture

Traditional
Arr. by Lyndell Leatherman

1. It's good to give thanks to the Lord._____ It's
2. It's good to give thanks for our *food._____ It's
3. God cares a - bout **you ev - ery day._____ God
4. The Lord is my Help - er each day._____ The

good to give thanks to the Lord._____ It's good to give thanks,__ it's
good to give thanks for our *food._____ It's good to give thanks,__ it's
cares a - bout **you ev - ery day._____ God cares a - bout you,__ God
Lord is my Help - er each day._____ The Lord is my Help - er, the

good to give thanks,__ It's good to give thanks to the Lord._____
good to give thanks,__ It's good to give thanks for our *food._____
cares a - bout you,__ God cares a - bout **you ev - ery day._____
Lord is my Help - er, The Lord is my Help - er each day._____

*Substitute names of other things for which children may thank God, such as legs, arms, family members, etc.
**Substitute child's name.

9 I Love Jesus

Words and Music by
EVELYN BEALS

Je-sus is my best friend; I love Him. Je-sus is my best friend; I love Him. Je-sus is my best friend; I love Him. I love Je-sus.

10 This Is God's House

L. M. OGLEVEE

W. G. OGLEVEE

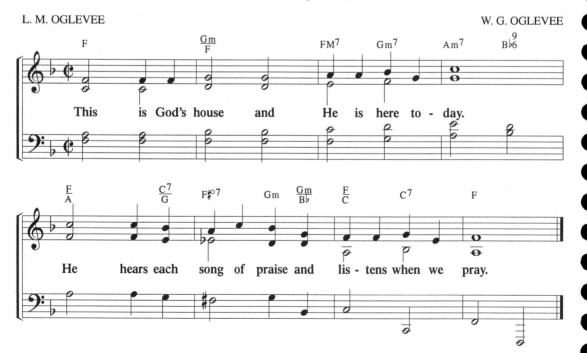

This is God's house and He is here to-day. He hears each song of praise and lis-tens when we pray.

God Hears My Prayer

MILDRED SPEAKES EDWARDS

Old French Melody
Arr. by Mildred Speakes Edwards
and Lyndell Leatherman

Motions:
1. Point upward.
2. Cup hands behind ears.
3. Fold hands.
4. Motion outward.
5. Motion outward with other hand.
6. Point upward.
7. Cup hands behind ears.
8. Fold hands.
9. Cup hands behind ears.
10. Cross hands
    diagonally over chest.
11. Point to lips.

12

We Go to Church

Traditional

This is the way we *go to church, Go to church, go to church. This is the way we go to church Ear-ly on Sun - day morn - ing.

*Substitute: sing in church, pray in church, sit in church, walk in church, etc.

13

When to Church I Go

CAROLINE KELLOGG

DOROTHY WEST

Ver - y soft - ly I will walk; Ver - y gent - ly I will talk
Tho' I can - not see Him there, God is with me ev - ery - where;

From *Kindergarten Songs and Rhythms*, 1954. Published by the
American Baptist Board of Education and Publication, Judson Press.

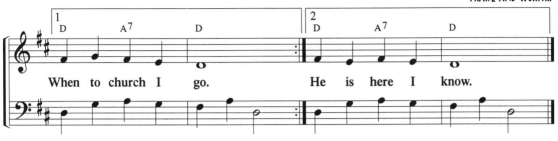

When to church I go. He is here I know.

Hush!

Traditional

Hush, lit-tle roos-ter with your cock-a-doo-dle-doo; Hush, lit-tle

kit-ten with your mew, mew, mew. Hush, pup-py dog with your

bow-wow-wow; Please don't moo-moo, Mis-sus Cow. Hush!

Hush! Hush! *Tim-my is talk-ing to God just now.

*Substitute other children's names or "We are talking . . ."

15

Jesus, Dear Jesus

Words and Music by
BONNIE COMPTON HANSON

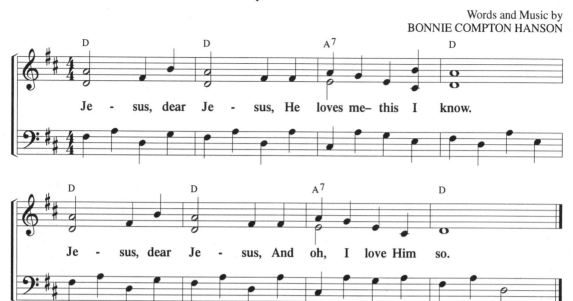

Je - sus, dear Je - sus, He loves me– this I know.

Je - sus, dear Je - sus, And oh, I love Him so.

16

With My Voice

Words and Music by
JOYCE GRIFFITTS

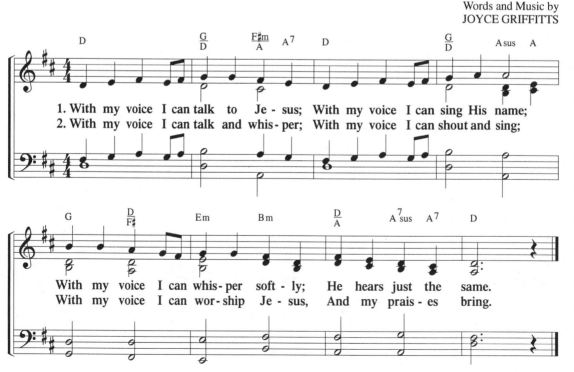

1. With my voice I can talk to Je - sus; With my voice I can sing His name;
2. With my voice I can talk and whis - per; With my voice I can shout and sing;

With my voice I can whis - per soft - ly; He hears just the same.
With my voice I can wor - ship Je - sus, And my prais - es bring.

God Made Our Wonderful World

Words and Music by
LENA S. LAWRENCE

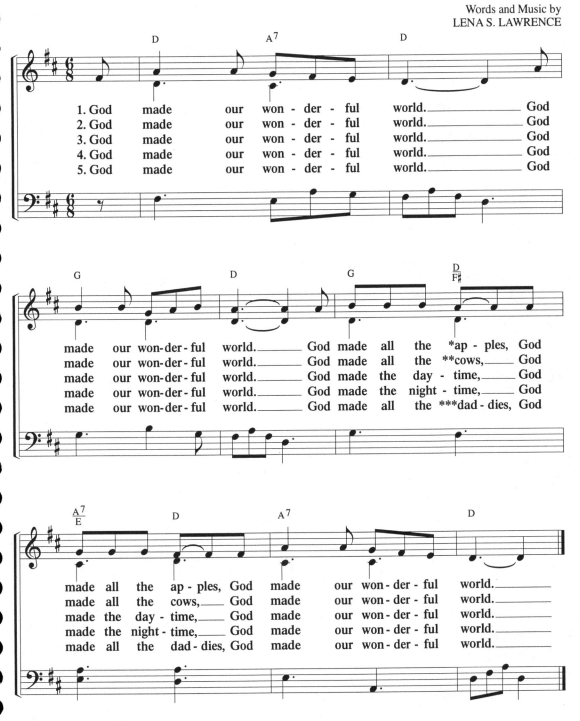

1. God made our won-der-ful world._____ God made our won-der-ful world._____ God made all the *ap-ples, God made all the ap-ples, God made our won-der-ful world._____
2. God made our won-der-ful world._____ God made our won-der-ful world._____ God made all the **cows,_____ God made all the cows,_____ God made our won-der-ful world._____
3. God made our won-der-ful world._____ God made our won-der-ful world._____ God made the day-time,_____ God made the day-time,_____ God made our won-der-ful world._____
4. God made our won-der-ful world._____ God made our won-der-ful world._____ God made the night-time,_____ God made the night-time,_____ God made our won-der-ful world._____
5. God made our won-der-ful world._____ God made our won-der-ful world._____ God made all the ***dad-dies, God made all the dad-dies, God made our won-der-ful world._____

*Substitute names of familiar foods.
**Substitute names of familiar animals.
***Substitute other family members.

Verses 1-3 on recording.

18
God's Care

Words and Music by
CLAUDE and CAROLYN RHEA

1. Look - ing all a - round,___ I see Just how
2. Taught the flow - ers how___ to grow, Showed the
3. Paint - ed grass a love - ly green, Told the

much God cares___ for me. He pro - vides for
wind just how___ to blow— He's the One who
rain to keep earth clean, Gave each bird a

ev - ery need. He cre - at - ed ev - ery___ seed.
made___ life start, Plant - ed love with - in___ my___ heart.
song___ to sing, Shows His love in ev - ery - thing.

19
God Made Everything

MABETH CLEM

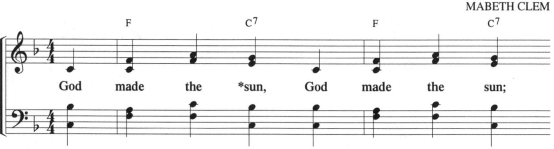

God made the *sun, God made the sun;

*Substitute: moon, stars, day, night, trees, flowers, wind, sea, rain, snow.

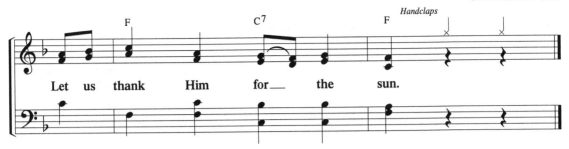

Let us thank Him for— the sun.

If I Were the Wind

20

Words and Music by
MYRA MARSHALL

1. If I were *the wind,——— how would I sound? If
2. God made the world and all these—— things.———

I were the wind,——— how would I sound? If
God made the world and all these—— things.———

I were the wind,——— how would I sound?
God made the world and all— these things.

Oo——— Oo——— That's how I'd sound.
Thank You, thank You, Thank You, dear God.

*Substitute: a duck . . . quack; a bird . . . chirp; an owl . . . hoo, etc.

21 God Gave Me Eyes

Words and Music by
MARGARET L. CRAIN

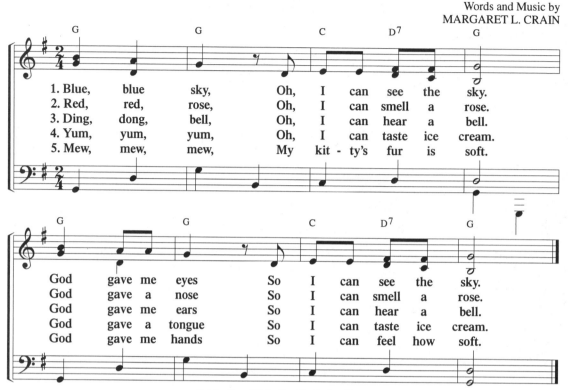

1. Blue, blue sky, Oh, I can see the sky.
2. Red, red, rose, Oh, I can smell a rose.
3. Ding, dong, bell, Oh, I can hear a bell.
4. Yum, yum, yum, Oh, I can taste ice cream.
5. Mew, mew, mew, My kit-ty's fur is soft.

God gave me eyes So I can see the sky.
God gave a nose So I can smell a rose.
God gave me ears So I can hear a bell.
God gave a tongue So I can taste ice cream.
God gave me hands So I can feel how soft.

Originally published by The Judson Press.

22 What a Wonderful World

Words and Music by
WILLIAM J. REYNOLDS

What a won-der-ful, won-der-ful, won-der-ful world God
made for you and me. A won-der-ful world, a won-der-ful world, What a

won-der-ful place to be, _____ A won-der-ful place to be.

All Things Bright and Beautiful

23

CECIL FRANCES ALEXANDER

Adapted from a Danish Folk Song
Arr. by Lyndell Leatherman

Each lit-tle flow'r that o - pens,   Each lit-tle bird that
made their glow-ing col - ors;   He made their ti - ny

sings–   God   wings.   Yes,   all   things bright   and

beau-ti-ful,   All   crea-tures great and   small,   And   all   things

wise   and   won-der-ful–   The   Lord   God   made   them   all.

24

I Often Think of God

Words and Music by
CARL PERRY

1. When I see a star twink-ling in the night, I of-ten think of God. When I see the moon so___ big and bright, I of-ten think of God.
2. When I hear a bird be-gin to sing, I of-ten think of God. When I see a bee with its ti-ny wings, I of-ten think of God.

Option: Teacher sing first phrase; children sing "I often think of God."

25

God's Night Light

Words and Music by
JOAN E. FOWLER

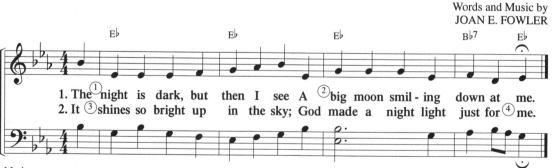

1. The ①night is dark, but then I see A ②big moon smil-ing down at me.
2. It ③shines so bright up in the sky; God made a night light just for ④me.

Motions:
1. Cover eyes with hands.
2. Make circle with arms above head.
3. Point to sky.
4. Point to self.

Nighttime Thoughts

EVELYN J. BEALS

Old French Air
Arr. by Lyndell Leatherman

1. Twin - kle, twin - kle, lit - tle star— How I won - der
2. It is dark and night is here, But I know that

what you are. God has put you in the sky,
God is near. When I say my eve - ning prayer,

And some - times I won - der why. But I'm glad you're
I know God is ev - ery - where. When I close my

shin - ing there; You re - mind me of God's care.
eyes to sleep, I know God will safe - ly keep.

27

God Is Watching over You

Words and Music by
RICK POWELL

God is watch-ing o-ver you, Watch-ing o-ver you, watch-ing o-ver you. God is watch-ing o-ver you, Watch-ing o-ver you each day.

28

Wonder Song

GRACE W. OWENS   CLARA LEE PARKER

1. Oh, who can make a flow-er? I'm sure I can't, can you? Oh,
2. Oh, who can make the rain-drops? I'm sure I can't, can you? Oh,
3. Oh, who can make the sun-shine? I'm sure I can't, can you? Oh,
4. Oh, who can make a butter-fly? I'm sure I can't, can you? Oh,
5. Oh, who can make the wind blow? I'm sure I can't, can you? Oh,

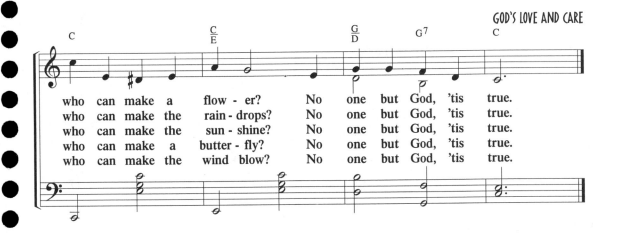

who can make a flow - er? No one but God, 'tis true.
who can make the rain - drops? No one but God, 'tis true.
who can make the sun - shine? No one but God, 'tis true.
who can make a butter - fly? No one but God, 'tis true.
who can make the wind blow? No one but God, 'tis true.

I Have a Friend

29

Words and Music by
HOMER A. RODEHEAVER

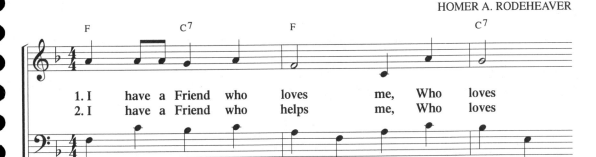

1. I have a Friend who loves me, Who loves
2. I have a Friend who helps me, Who loves

me, who loves me. I have a Friend who
me, who helps me. I have a Friend who

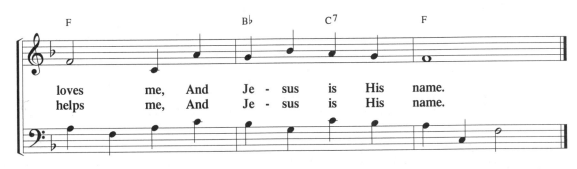

loves me, And Je - sus is His name.
helps me, And Je - sus is His name.

30 Jesus Loves the Little Children

Unknown

GEORGE F. ROOT

Je - sus loves the lit - tle chil - dren, All the chil-dren of the world. Red and yel - low, black and white, They are pre - cious in His sight; Je - sus loves the lit - tle chil - dren of the world.

31 God Is So Good

Unknown

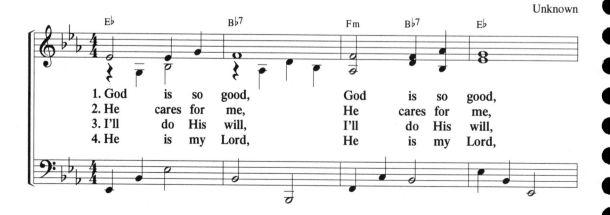

1. God is so good, God is so good,
2. He cares for me, He cares for me,
3. I'll do His will, I'll do His will,
4. He is my Lord, He is my Lord,

God   is   so   good,   He's   so   good   to   me.
He   cares for me,   He's   so   good   to   me.
I'll   do   His will,   He's   so   good   to   me.
He   is   my   Lord,   He's   so   good   to   me.

Jesus Loves the Little Ones

32

Traditional
Arr. by Lyndell Leatherman

1. Je - sus loves the lit - tle ones like me, me, me.   Je - sus loves the
2. Je - sus loves the lit - tle ones like you, you, you. Je - sus loves the

lit - tle ones like me, me, me.   Lit - tle ones like me
lit - tle ones like you, you, you. Lit - tle ones like you

sat   up - on His knee.   Je - sus loves the lit - tle ones like me, me, me.
saves them thro' and thro';   Je - sus loves the lit - tle ones like you, you, you.

33

God Tells Me

Words and Music by
BONNIE COMPTON HANSON

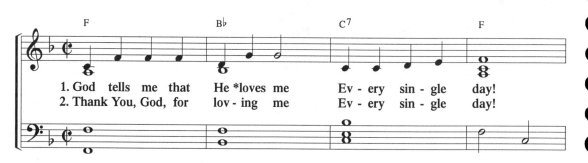

1. God tells me that He *loves me Ev - ery sin - gle day!
2. Thank You, God, for lov - ing me Ev - ery sin - gle day!

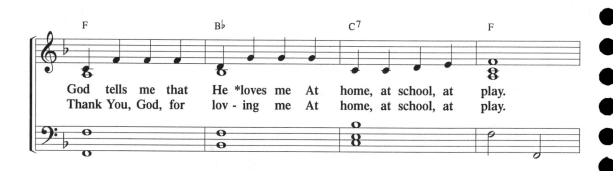

God tells me that He *loves me At home, at school, at play.
Thank You, God, for lov - ing me At home, at school, at play.

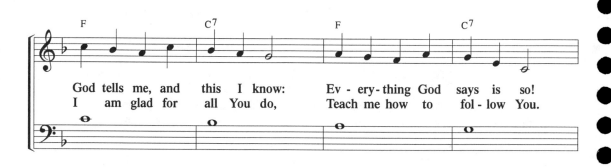

God tells me, and this I know: Ev - ery-thing God says is so!
I am glad for all You do, Teach me how to fol - low You.

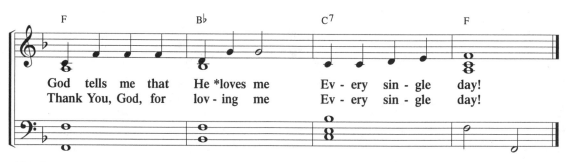

God tells me that He *loves me Ev - ery sin - gle day!
Thank You, God, for lov - ing me Ev - ery sin - gle day!

*Substitute: hears, helps.

Zaccheus

Traditional

① Zac - chae - us was a wee lit - tle man, ② A wee lit - tle man was he. ③ He climbed up in a syc - a - more tree, ④ For the Lord he want - ed to see. ⑤ And as the Sav - ior passed that way, He looked up in the tree; ⑥ *And He said:* "Zaccheus, you come down! For I'm go - ing to your house to - day, For I'm go - ing to your house to - day."

Spoken:

Motions:
1. Hands in front, right palm raised above left palm.
2. Move palms closer together.
3. Alternate hands in climbing motion.
4. Shade eyes with right hand and look down.
5. Shade eyes with right hand and look up.
6. Look up, gesture to Zaccheus to come down.
7. Clap hands on accented beats.

35 The Bible Tells Us Jesus Grew

ROY T. SCROGGINS, JR.

English Folk Melody
Arr. by Roy T. Scroggins, Jr.

1. The Bi - ble tells___ us Je - sus grew In
2. The Bi - ble tells___ us Je - sus grew In
3. The Bi - ble tells___ us Je - sus grew In

ways that you___ and I grow, too. Tall - er, strong - er,
ways that you___ and I grow, too. Learn - ing, think - ing,
ways that you___ and I grow, too. Car - ing, help - ing,

ev - ery day, He liked to work___ and help and play.
be - ing kind, His mind was grow - ing just like mine.
ev - ery day, He showed God's love___ in ev - ery way.

36 I Open My Bible and Read

Words and Music by
PHEROBA THOMAS

I o - pen my Bi - ble and read: *"God loves me."___

*Substitute: "Jesus healed the sick"; "Be ye kind"; "God made me"; etc.
Option: For stronger reinforcement of ideas, sing each verse twice.

Noah

PAUL WILLIAMS

PAUL and DONNA WILLIAMS

1. No - ah, No - ah, Put the an - i - mals in the
2. Rain came, rain came, But the an - i - mals all were
3. Sun came, sun came, So the an - i - mals left the

ark.   ark.   They went in two by
safe.   safe.   The wa - ter rose up
ark.   ark.   They went out two by

two,   Gi - raffe and kan - ga - roo.   No - ah,
high;   In - side the ark was dry.   Rain came,
two,   Gi - raffe and kan - ga - roo.   Sun came,

No - ah,   Put the an - i - mals in the ark.
rain came,   But the an - i - mals all were safe.
sun came,   So the an - i - mals left the ark.

Option: Create an "ark" by arranging chairs in the shape of a boat (with room in the middle).
Designate a "door," appoint a "Noah," and assign animal roles to the rest of the children.
Vs. 1: "Noah" leads "animals" into the "ark." Vs. 2: All stand inside the "ark." Vs. 3: "Noah" leads "animals" out of the "ark."

38

A Happy Home

SUZANNE H. CLASON

Traditional

1. God told us how to have a hap-py home, Have a hap-py
2. God said, "O-bey your par-ents in the Lord. Do just as they
3. God said, "Be kind to oth-ers in your home, Oth-ers in your

home, have a hap-py home. God told us how to
say; mind them ev-ery day." God said, "O-bey your
home, oth-ers in your home." God said, "Be kind to

have a hap-py home, And___ live for Him each day.
par-ents and you'll have A___ long life in My land."
oth-ers in your home, And be hap-py ev-ery day."

39

Friends of God

Words and Music by
LINDA J. BURBA

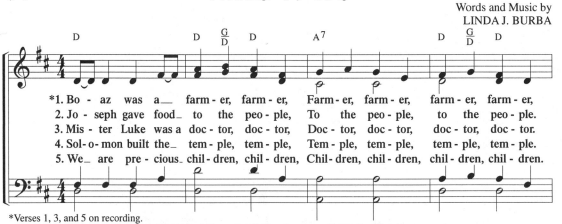

*1. Bo - az was a_ farm-er, farm-er, Farm-er, farm-er, farm-er, farm-er,
2. Jo - seph gave food_ to the peo-ple, To the peo-ple, to the peo-ple.
3. Mis - ter Luke was a doc-tor, doc-tor, Doc-tor, doc-tor, doc-tor, doc-tor.
4. Sol-o-mon built the_ tem-ple, tem-ple, Tem-ple, tem-ple, tem-ple, tem-ple.
5. We_ are pre-cious_ chil-dren, chil-dren, Chil-dren, chil-dren, chil-dren, chil-dren.

*Verses 1, 3, and 5 on recording.

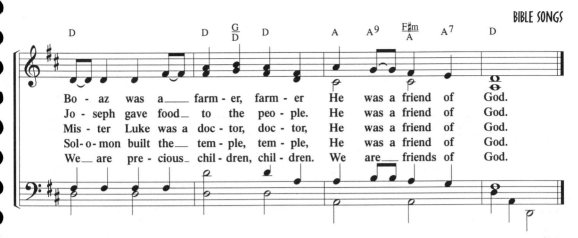

Bo - az was a___ farm - er, farm - er He was a friend of God.
Jo - seph gave food_ to the peo - ple. He was a friend of God.
Mis - ter Luke was a doc - tor, doc - tor, He was a friend of God.
Sol - o - mon built the_ tem - ple, tem - ple, He was a friend of God.
We_ are pre - cious_ chil - dren, chil - dren. We are_ friends of God.

Let the Children Come to Me

40

C. DENISE YOUNG   Traditional

"Let the chil - dren come to Me, Come to Me, come to Me.

Let the chil - dren come to Me," That's what Je - sus said._____ In

Mat - thew nine - teen, four - teen, In Mat - thew nine - teen, four - teen,

"Let the chil - dren come to Me," That's what Je - sus said.

41

Hinges

Traditional

1. I'm all made of hing-es, and ev-ery-thing bends From the
2. I'm glad that God made me so I can do things Like___

top of my head 'way down to my ends. I'm hing-es in front and I'm
play-ing with toys and sit-ting in swings. It's fun to bend o-ver and

hing-es in back; If I did-n't have hing-es, I sure-ly would crack.
sit on the floor, And_ hing-es al-low me to do this and more.

42

Hands on Shoulders

Unknown

1. Hands on shoul-ders, hands on knees, Hands be-y-
2. Hands 'way up high in the air; At your

Follow the motions as suggested by the words of the song.

hind you, if you please. Touch your shoul - ders,
sides, then touch your hair. Hands 'way up high

touch your nose, Touch your hair___ and touch your toes.
as be - fore; Clap your hands,___ one, two, three, four.

The Wiggle Song

43

Traditional

1. My thumbs are start - ing to wig - gle, My thumbs are
2. My thumbs and fin - gers are wig - gling, My thumbs and

start - ing to wig - gle, My thumbs are start - ing to
fin - gers are wig - gling, My thumbs and fin - gers are

wig - gle A - round, a - round, a - round.___
wig - gling A - round, a - round, a - round.___

Additional verses:
3. My hand is starting to wiggle . . .
4. My arms are starting to wiggle . . .
5. My head is satrting to wiggle . . .
6. Now all of me is a-wiggling . . .

44 Things That I Can Do

Words and Music by
DERRELL BILLINGSLY

1. There are man - y things that I can do;
2. There are man - y things that I can do;
3. There are man - y sounds that I can make;

Doo - dle, doo - dle, doot, doot, doo. I can sing a song with
Doo - dle, doo - dle, doot, doot, doo. I can play a song with
Doo - dle, doo - dle, doot, doot, doo. I can make a sound just

notes so true: Doo - dle, doo - dle, doot, doot, doo.
in - stru - ments: *(Play instruments to the steady beat.)*
like a *cow: Moo, moo, moo, moo, moo, moo, moo.

*Substitute: sheep . . . baa; duck . . . quack; etc.

45 Open, Shut Them

Traditional
Arr. by Lyndell Leatherman

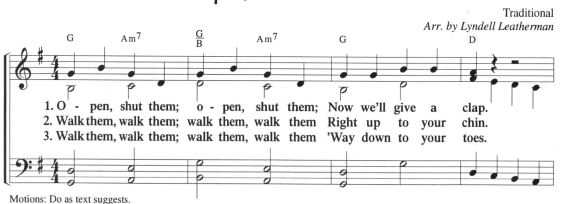

1. O - pen, shut them; o - pen, shut them; Now we'll give a clap.
2. Walk them, walk them; walk them, walk them Right up to your chin.
3. Walk them, walk them; walk them, walk them 'Way down to your toes.

Motions: Do as text suggests.

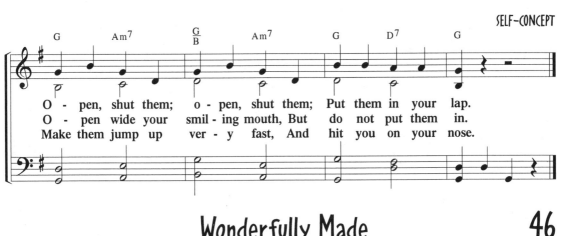

Wonderfully Made

46

Words and Music by
CLAUDE and CAROLYN RHEA

Exercise Song

Words and Music by
CLAUDE and CAROLYN RHEA

One, two, three, kick. One, two, three, jump.

One, two, three, touch the floor._____

One, two, three, stretch. One, two, three, clap.

One, two, three, jump some more._____

Motions: Do as text suggests.

To prepare the children to sit quietly for a Bible story, you could use the following words:
One, two, three, smile.
One, two, three, bow.
One, two, three, turn around.
Lift your chin high.
Take a deep breath.
Now let us all sit down.

Head and Shoulders, Knees and Toes

48

Unknown

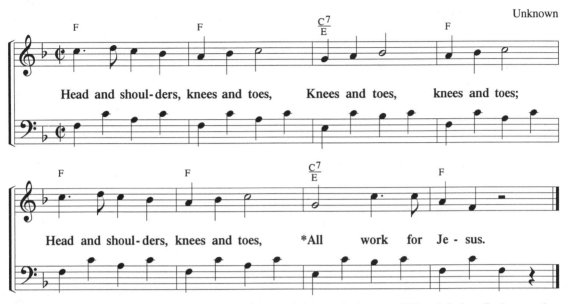

Head and shoul-ders, knees and toes, Knees and toes, knees and toes;

Head and shoul-ders, knees and toes, *All work for Je-sus.

Motions: As each part of the body is mentioned, have children touch that part. On the phrase, "All work for Jesus," point upward.

*"Clap your hands and praise Him" is an alternate last phrase.

Cheerfully Obey

49

BEA BAILEY

DWIGHT UPHAUS

1. I know that Je-sus wants me to cheer-ful-ly o - bey; And
2. It is - n't al-ways eas - y to cheer-ful-ly o - bey; But

I will try to please Him_____ in things I do and say.
since I want to please Him,_____ I'll do it an - y - way.

50

God Needs Helpers

KATHRYN BLACKBURN PECK

FAITH CHAMBERS WILSON

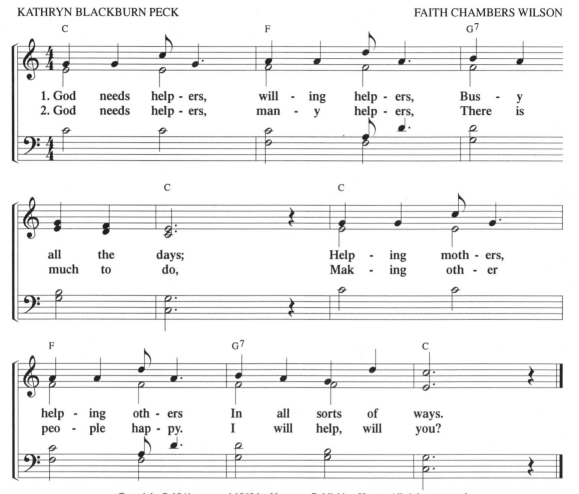

1. God needs help- ers, will- ing help- ers, Bus- y
2. God needs help- ers, man- y help- ers, There is

all the days; Help- ing moth- ers,
much to do, Mak- ing oth- er

help- ing oth- ers In all sorts of ways.
peo- ple hap- py. I will help, will you?

51

A Friend

Words and Music by
LAWRENCE O. RICHARDS

1. A ①friend loves at all times; ②A good friend I'll be. So
2. A ①friend is a help- er; ②A good friend I'll be. So

Motions:
1. Nod head.
2. Point to self while nodding head.
3. Gesture to include the group.
4. Point upward.

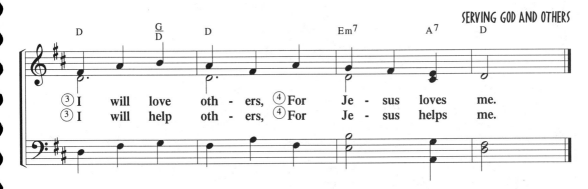

③ I will love oth - ers, ④ For Je - sus loves me.
③ I will help oth - ers, ④ For Je - sus helps me.

Take the Blame

Words and Music by
CLAUDE and CAROLYN RHEA

1. I must learn to take the blame And if I'm wrong, ad -
2. If I take what is - n't mine, Then sure - ly I'll ad -

mit it. ③ It would real - ly be a
mit it. That's the on - ly way to

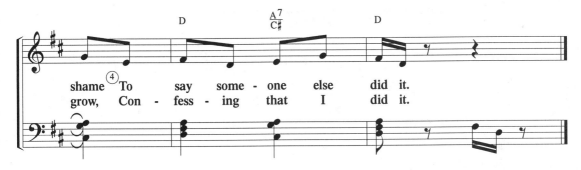

shame ④ To say some - one else did it.
grow, Con - fess - ing that I did it.

Motions:
1. Point to self.
2. Shake finger for emphasis and nod head "yes."
3. Shake head "no" sadly.
4. Continue shaking head and point to another person.

53 A Helper I Will Be

VALERIE A. WILSON

Traditional

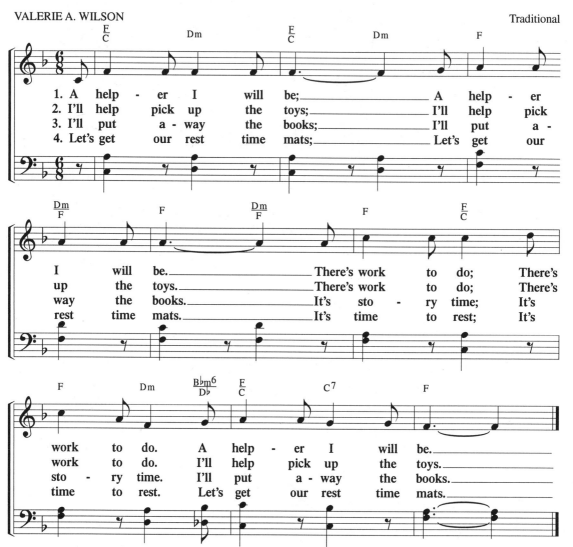

1. A help-er I will be;_____ A help-er
2. I'll help pick up the toys;_____ I'll help pick
3. I'll put a-way the books;_____ I'll put a-
4. Let's get our rest time mats;_____ Let's get our

I will be._____ There's work to do; There's
up the toys._____ There's work to do; There's
way the books._____ It's sto-ry time; It's
rest time mats._____ It's time to rest; It's

work to do. A help-er I will be._____
work to do. I'll help pick up the toys._____
sto-ry time. I'll put a-way the books._____
time to rest. Let's get our rest time mats._____

54 Jesus, the Helper

Words and Music by
NATHAN CORBITT

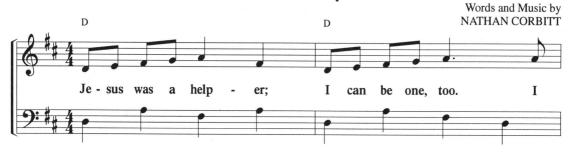

Je-sus was a help-er; I can be one, too. I

help my *dad - dy rake the leaves and I'm a help - er, too.

*Substitute: mommy clean the house, sister pick up toys, brother wash the car, teacher sing a song.

Children, Obey Your Parents

55

Words and Music by
GERALD R. CARTER

1. Chil - dren, o - bey your *par - ents,
2. We can be kind and help - ful,

This makes a hap - pi - er home.
This makes a hap - pi - er home.

Chil - dren, o - bey your par - ents,
We can be kind and help - ful,

This makes a hap - pi - er home.
This makes a hap - pi - er home.

*Substitute: father, mother

56

Special Words

Words and Music by
TALMADGE BUTLER

There are spe-cial words that we should know; We should use them wher-ev-er we go: "Please" and "I'm sor-ry," "Par-don me" and "thank you." These are spe-cial words. These are spe-cial words.

57

When Friends Come

Words and Music by
JOY LATHAM

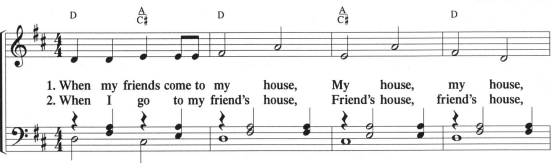

1. When my friends come to my house, My house, my house,
2. When I go to my friend's house, Friend's house, my friend's house,

*Substitute: I will share my toys, we'll take turns and share, we'll have a happy time.

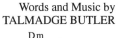

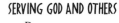

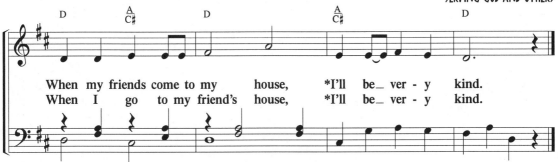

When my friends come to my house, *I'll be— ver - y kind.
When I go to my friend's house, *I'll be— ver - y kind.

*Substitute: I will share my toys, we'll take turns and share, we'll have a happy time.

Helping God

58

Words and Music by
CLAUDE and CAROLYN RHEA

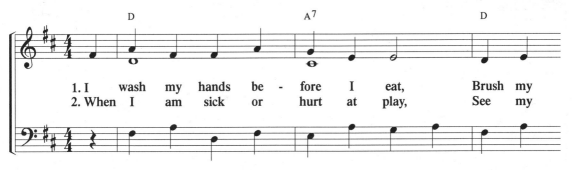

1. I wash my hands be - fore I eat, Brush my
2. When I am sick or hurt at play, See my

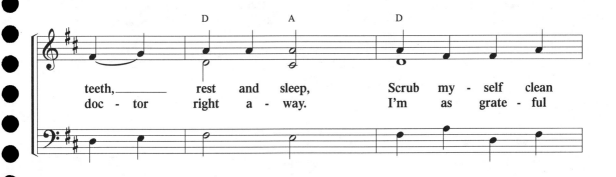

teeth,_____ rest and sleep, Scrub my - self clean
doc - tor right a - way. I'm as grate - ful

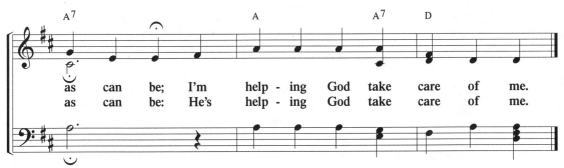

as can be; I'm help - ing God take care of me.
as can be; He's help - ing God take care of me.

59

O Be Careful

Traditional
Arr. by Lyndell Leatherman

With a shuffle

1. O be care-ful, lit-tle eyes, what you see; O be care-ful, lit-tle eyes, what you see; For the Fa-ther up a-bove Is look-ing down in love; So be care-ful, lit-tle eyes, what you see.
2. O be care-ful, lit-tle ears, what you hear; O be care-ful, lit-tle ears, what you hear; For the Fa-ther up a-bove Is look-ing down in love; So be care-ful, lit-tle ears, what you hear.
3. O be care-ful, lit-tle tongue, what you say; O be care-ful, lit-tle tongue, what you say; For the Fa-ther up a-bove Is look-ing down in love; So be care-ful, lit-tle tongue, what you say.
4. O be care-ful, lit-tle hands, what you do; O be care-ful, lit-tle hands, what you do; For the Fa-ther up a-bove Is look-ing down in love; So be care-ful, lit-tle hands, what you do.
5. O be care-ful, lit-tle feet, where you go; O be care-ful, lit-tle feet, where you go; For the Fa-ther up a-bove Is look-ing down in love; So be care-ful, lit-tle feet, where you go.

*Verses 1-3, 5 on recording.

Motions: Point to the part of the body mentioned in each verse.

This Is My Prayer

Words and Music by
DOUG HOLCK

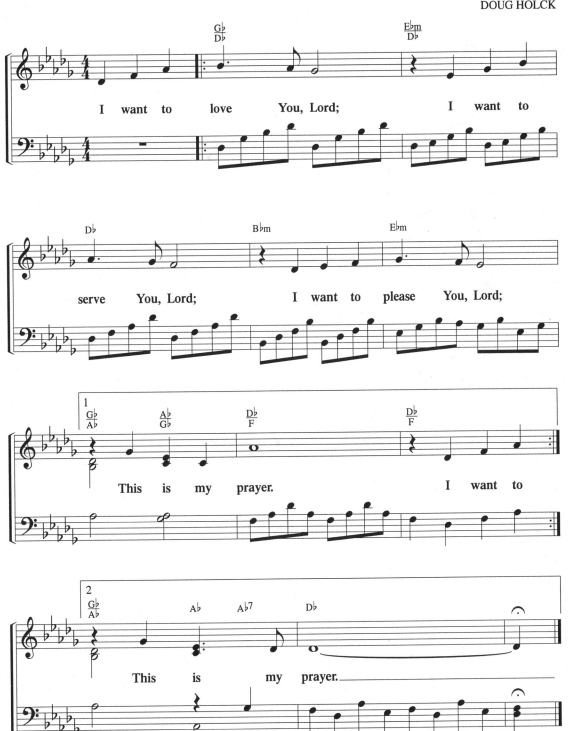

61 Missionaries

Words and Music by
CLAUDE and CAROLYN RHEA

Mis - sion - ar - ies tell of Je - sus 'Round the world ev - ery - where. I can help them with my mon - ey; I can help them with my prayer.

62 Giving

MARY LeBAR

A. VIVIENNE BLOMQUIST
Arr. by Lyndell Leatherman

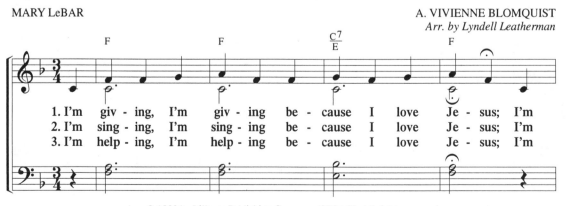

1. I'm giv - ing, I'm giv - ing be - cause I love Je - sus; I'm
2. I'm sing - ing, I'm sing - ing be - cause I love Je - sus; I'm
3. I'm help - ing, I'm help - ing be - cause I love Je - sus; I'm

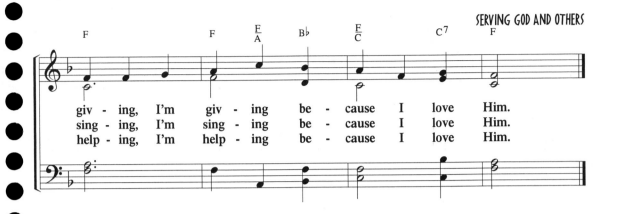

giv - ing, I'm giv - ing be - cause I love Him.
sing - ing, I'm sing - ing be - cause I love Him.
help - ing, I'm help - ing be - cause I love Him.

Little Children

63

Words and Music by
CAROL M. DETTONI

Lit - tle chil - dren *in Mex - i - co, Je - sus loves

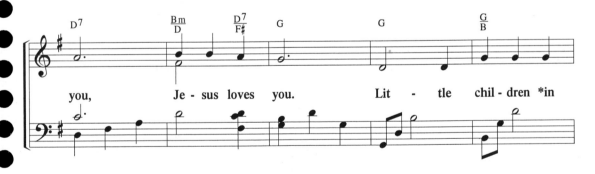

you, Je - sus loves you. Lit - tle chil - dren *in

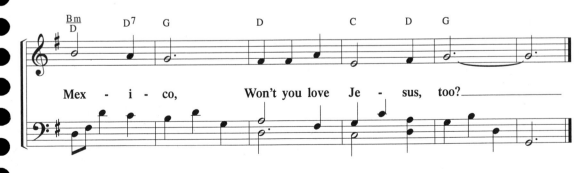

Mex - i - co, Won't you love Je - sus, too?_____

*Substitute: in Africa, in India, in far Japan, across the sea, etc. "In Mexico" and "across the sea" verses on recording.
Copyright © 1962 Gospel Light Publications. Used by permission.

64

Thanksgiving Day

Words and Music by
MYRA MARSHALL

Thanks-giv-ing Day is a hap-py day, *And we say, "Thank You, God." Thanks-giv-ing Day is a hap-py day, *And we say, "Thank You, God."

*Substitute: with turkey and pumpkin pie, we go to Grandma's house, etc.

65

I'm Happy Today

VALERIE A. WILSON

MERYL E. WELCH

I'm hap-py, I'm hap-py, I'm hap-py to-day;

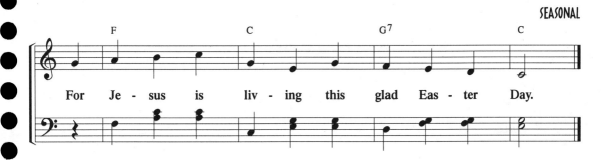

For Je - sus is liv - ing this glad Eas - ter Day.

Hosanna!

66

Traditional

*Ho - san - na! Ho - san - na! All the

peo - ple sing._____ Ho - san - na! Ho -

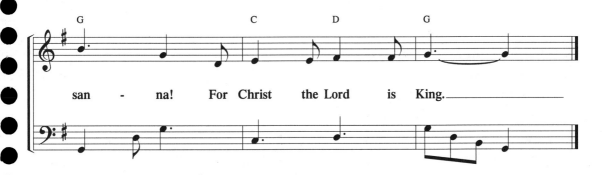

san - na! For Christ the Lord is King._____

*"Hosanna" means "save, we pray." Originally, "hosanna" was a one-word Hebrew
 prayer of deliverance (Ps. 118:25). It later recurred as a praise or blessing for Jesus.

67

Merry Christmas

Words and Music by
RICHARD C. BERG
Arr. by Lyndell Leatherman

*1. Mer-ry Christ-mas, mer-ry Christ-mas, And a hap-py,
2. Hap-py Eas-ter, hap-py Eas-ter; Christ a-rose and

hap-py new year! Mer-ry Christ-mas, mer-ry
lives to - day. Hap-py Eas - ter, hap-py

Christ-mas, And a hap - py, hap - py new year!
Eas-ter, Christ a-rose and lives to - day.

*Verse 1 on recording.
Option: Substitute special moments or occasions such as: Happy birthday, happy birthday,
you're six years old today; It's snowing, it's snowing, we'll play in snow today!

68

Baby Jesus

Words and Music by
NATHAN CORBITT

1. Je - sus in a man - ger lay In a sta - ble low - ly.
2. Shep - herds came to see the Child In a sta - ble low - ly.

Je - sus in a man - ger lay On a cold, cold night.
Shep - herds came to see the Child On a cold, cold night.

Song for Special Days

69

Words and Music by
CLAUDE and CAROLYN RHEA

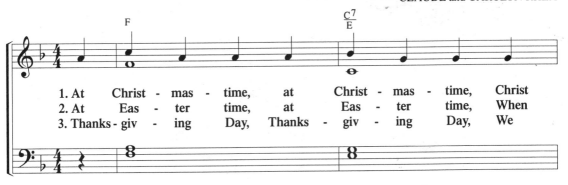

1. At Christ - mas - time, at Christ - mas - time, Christ
2. At Eas - ter time, at Eas - ter time, When
3. Thanks - giv - ing Day, Thanks - giv - ing Day, We

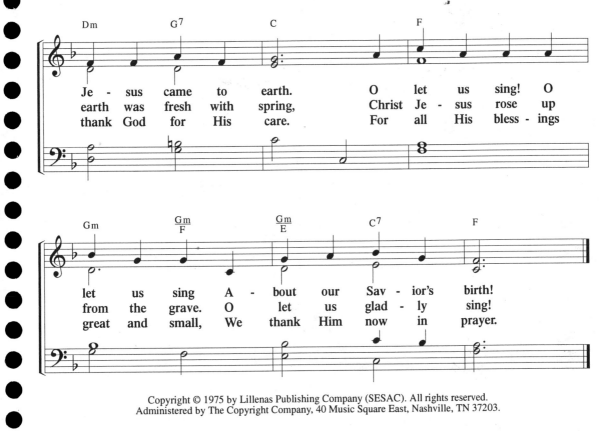

Je - sus came to earth. O let us sing! O
earth was fresh with spring, Christ Je - sus rose up
thank God for His care. For all His bless - ings

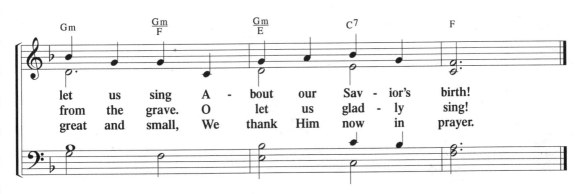

let us sing A - bout our Sav - ior's birth!
from the grave. O let us glad - ly sing!
great and small, We thank Him now in prayer.

O Come, Little Children

Traditional

O come, lit-tle chil-dren; O come, one and all! O come to the man-ger in Beth-le-hem's stall And see Ba-by Je-sus a-sleep on the hay. He came to bring joy to all chil-dren to-day.

Away in a Manger

Anonymous

JAMES R. MURRAY

Suggested motions for verse 1:

1. Fold arms as though holding a baby and make rocking motions.
2. Lay head on folded hands.
3. Point upward.
4. Place hand as though shading eyes and look down.

72 Christ Was Born in Bethlehem

Adapted by EUNICE BOARDMAN

Early American Hymn
Arr. by Lyndell Leatherman

*1. Christ was born in Beth - le-hem, Christ was born in Beth - le-hem,
2. Mar - y was in Beth - le-hem, Mar - y was in Beth - le-hem,
3. Jo - seph was in Beth - le-hem, Jo - seph was in Beth - le-hem,
4. An - gels sang in Beth - le-hem, An - gels sang in Beth - le-hem,
5. Shep - herds came to Beth - le-hem, Shep - herds came to Beth - le-hem,

Christ was born in Beth - le-hem And in the man - ger lay. And
Mar - y was in Beth - le-hem Up - on that Christ-mas Day. Up -
Jo - seph was in Beth - le-hem Up - on that Christ-mas Day. Up -
An - gels sang in Beth - le-hem Up - on that Christ-mas Day. Up -
Shep - herds came to Beth - le-hem Up - on that Christ-mas Day. Up -

in the man - ger lay, And in the man - ger lay.
on that Christ-mas Day, Up - on that Christ-mas Day.
on that Christ-mas Day, Up - on that Christ-mas Day.
on that Christ-mas Day, Up - on that Christ-mas Day.
on that Christ-mas Day, Up - on that Christ-mas Day.

*Verses 1, 4, and 5 on recording.

Option: When they have learned the words, invite the class to dramatize the song. Choose one child to be Mary and one to be Joseph. The remainder of the class may be shepherds and angels. Encourage the children to plan their own simple actions to represent the Christmas story as they know it.

Christ was born in Beth - le - hem And in the man - ger lay.
Mar - y was in Beth - le - hem Up - on that Christ-mas Day.
Jo - seph was in Beth - le - hem Up - on that Christ-mas Day.
An - gels sang in Beth - le - hem Up - on that Christ-mas Day.
Shep - herds came to Beth - le - hem Up - on that Christ-mas Day.

Baby Jesus

73

KATHRYN BLACKBURN PECK

FAITH CHAMBERS WILSON

1. Ba - by Je - sus went to sleep On a
2. Moth - er Mar - y tucked Him in, Warmed His

bed ___ of hay; In a man - ger
ti - ny feet; Sang a lul - la -

soft and deep Ba - by Je - sus lay.
by to Him, "Sleep, ___ my Ba - by, sleep."

We Were Made to Love the Lord

Words and Music by
KATHIE HILL and JANET MCMAHAN

*1. God made birds__ to fill the skies,_____ God made frogs to eat the flies,_____
2. God made fish__ to swim the seas,_____ God made squirrels to climb the trees,_____
*3. God made fox-es to be real_trick-y, God made worms to feel real_stick-y,

God made owls_____ to just look wise,__ But we were made to love the Lord.
God made dogs_____ to car-ry fleas,__ But we were made to love the Lord.
God made spi-ders to just be yick-y, But we were made to love the Lord.

Refrain

Yes, we were made to love the Lord,_____ Love the Lord,_____ love the Lord.

We were made to love the Lord;_____ That's what we were made for.

*Verses 1 and 3 on recording.

Say to the Lord, I Love You

Words and Music by
ERNIE RETTINO and DEBBY KERNER

Creature Praise

Words and Music by
DALE MATTHEWS

1. Large crea-tures, small crea-tures, short and tall crea-tures,
2. Low crea-tures, high crea-tures, fly-in' in the sky crea-tures, Come now and
3. Day crea-tures, night crea-tures, left and right crea-tures,

praise the Lord.

Young crea-tures, old crea-tures,
White crea-tures, brown crea-tures,
Near crea-tures, far crea-tures,

hot and cold crea-tures,
all the world a-round crea-tures, Come now and praise the Lord.
an-y-where you are crea-tures,

Refrain

Sing praise to the Fa-ther, sing praise to the

This Is the Day

Words and Music by
LES GARRETT

This is the day, this is the day That the Lord has made, that the
Lord has made. We will re-joice, we will re-joice And be
glad in it, and be glad in it. This is the day that the
Lord has made. We will re-joice and be glad in it.
This is the day, this is the day that the Lord has made.

Praise God, from Whom All Blessings Flow

78

THOMAS KEN

LOUIS BOURGEOIS

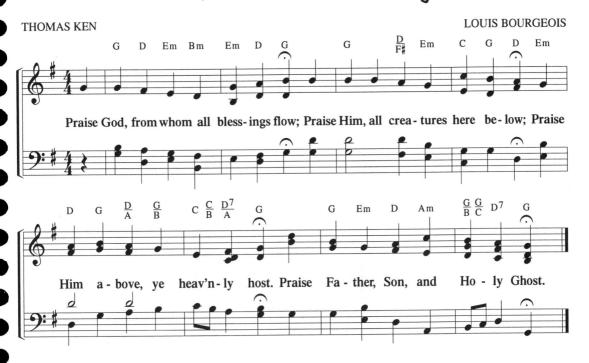

Praise God, from whom all bless-ings flow; Praise Him, all crea-tures here be-low; Praise
Him a-bove, ye heav'n-ly host. Praise Fa-ther, Son, and Ho-ly Ghost.

Jesus, I Love You

79

Words and Music by
OTIS SKILLINGS

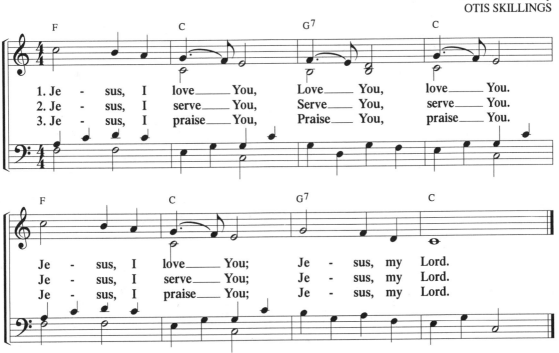

1. Je - sus, I love____ You,   Love____ You,   love____ You.
2. Je - sus, I serve____ You,   Serve____ You,   serve____ You.
3. Je - sus, I praise____ You, Praise____ You, praise____ You.

Je - sus, I love____ You;   Je - sus, my Lord.
Je - sus, I serve____ You;   Je - sus, my Lord.
Je - sus, I praise____ You; Je - sus, my Lord.

He Has Made Me Glad

Words and Music by
LEONA VON BRETHORST

I will en-ter His gates with thanks-giv-ing in my heart; I will en-ter His courts with praise;_____ I will say, "This is the day that the Lord has____ made." I will re-joice for He has made me glad._____ He has made me glad,

Lord, We Praise You

81

Words and Music by
OTIS SKILLINGS

1. Lord, we praise You. Lord, we praise You.
2. Lord, we love You. Lord, we love You.
3. Al - le - lu - ia! Al - le - lu - ia!

Lord, we praise You. We praise You, Lord.
Lord, we love You. We love You, Lord.
Al - le - lu - ia! We give You praise.

82

Hallelujah!

Traditional

He Is Lord

He is Lord; He is Lord. He is ris-en from the dead and He is Lord.

Ev-ery knee shall bow, ev-ery tongue con-fess That Je-sus Christ_is Lord.

Praise Him

*Praise_____Him, praise_____Him, Praise Him in the

morn-ing, Praise Him at the noon-time. Praise_____Him,

praise_____Him,_____ Praise Him when the sun goes down.

*Substitute: love Him, serve Him, thank Him

85 O How I Love Jesus

Anonymous

O how I love Je - sus. O how I love Je - sus.___ O how I love Je - sus, Be - cause___ He first loved me.

86 Gifts in My Heart

Words and Music by
BETSY HERNANDEZ

1. There are gifts in my heart, And I give them to the
2. More than dia - monds or gold Are the gifts that my heart
3. Though He owns all the stars, All the world and all there

87 Give Me Joy in My Heart

88 Everybody Ought to Love Jesus

Words and Music by
HARRY DIXON LOES

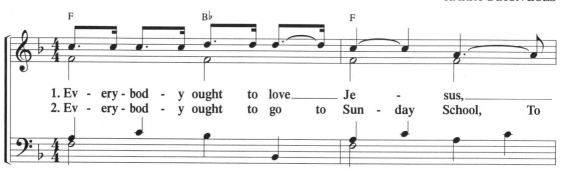

1. Ev - ery - bod - y ought to love Je - sus,
2. Ev - ery - bod - y ought to go to Sun - day School, To

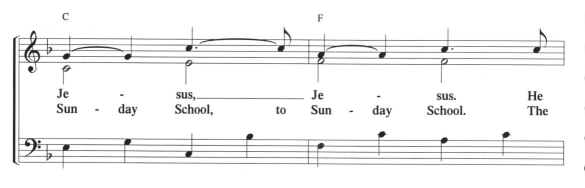

Je - sus, Je - sus. He
Sun - day School, to Sun - day School. The

died on the cross to save us from sin;
men and the wom - en and the boys and the girls;

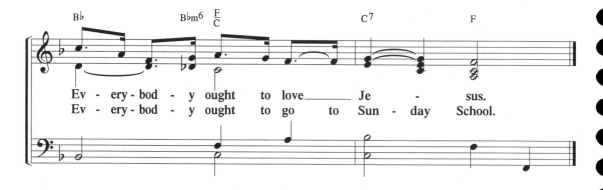

Ev - ery - bod - y ought to love Je - sus.
Ev - ery - bod - y ought to go to Sun - day School.

If You Can Sing a Song

Words and Music by
PETER and HANNEKE JACOBS

1,3. If you can sing a song, then praise the Lord. If you can
2. If you can reach up high, then praise the Lord, And try to

hum a-long, then praise the Lord. If you can sit down
reach the sky, then praise the Lord. Just like the green leaves

on the ground, Turn your bod-y all a-round, Or make a hap-py sound, praise the
on the tree, Sway-in' in the sum-mer breeze, Make a mel-o-dy to the

Lord. If you can make a hap-py sound, praise the Lord.
Lord. Just like the make a mel-o-dy to the Lord.

Option: Teacher may sing first part of phrases, with children joining in on "(then) praise the Lord."
Children would do according to the teacher's words.

You Are Lord to Me

Words and Music by
TOM MCLAIN

You are my Lord; You give life to me.

You give me hope; You're my Prince of Peace.

You cause the winds and the waves to cease;

You are Lord to me.

You are the Lord of glo-ry;

Father, I Adore You

*(Round)

91

Words and Music by
TERRYE COELHO

1. Fa - ther,
2. Je - sus, I a - dore You; Lay my life be -
3. Spir - it,

fore You. How I love You!

*The accompaniment is optional. When the song is sung as a round, the accompaniment should probably be omitted.

I Will Trust the Lord

Words and Music by
STEVE SCHALCHLIN

1. I will trust the Lord,_____ I will trust the Lord,
2. I will thank the Lord,_____ I will thank the Lord,
3. I will praise the Lord,_____ I will praise the Lord,
4. I will serve the Lord,_____ I will serve the Lord,

_____ I will trust the Lord_____ in
_____ I will thank the Lord_____ in
_____ I will praise the Lord_____ in
_____ I will serve the Lord_____ in

ev - ery - thing.
ev - ery - thing.
ev - ery - thing.
ev - ery - thing.   In

ev-ery-thing I will give thanks._____ In ev-ery-thing I will give thanks.

I will thank the Lord in ev - ery - thing.

What a Mighty God We Serve

93

Unknown
Arr. by Lyndell Leatherman

What a might - y God we serve.

What a might - y God we serve.

An - gels bow be - fore Him; Heav'n and earth a - dore Him.

What a might - y God we serve.

Answer Song

Words and Music by
SUZANNE H. CLASON

1. Who loves the Lord to-day?_____ I do, I do.
2. Does Je-sus save you now?_____ He does, He does.
3. Who will o-bey God's Word?_____ I will, I will.

Who loves the Lord to-day?_____ I do, I do.
Does Je-sus save you now?_____ He does, He does.
Who will o-bey God's Word?_____ I will, I will.

We love the Lord to-day,_____ We do, we do.

We love the Lord to-day._____ We love the Lord.

When We Talk to Him

Words and Music by
KEN BIBLE

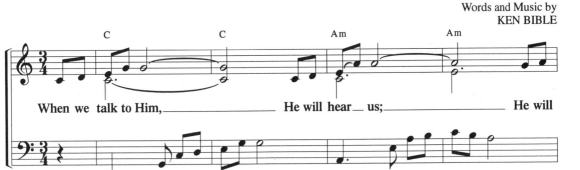

When we talk to Him, _____ He will hear __ us; _____ He will

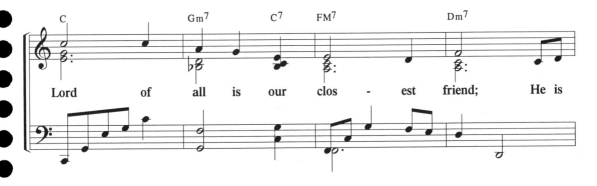

lis - ten to all that we say. _____ For the

Lord of all is our clos - est friend; He is

with us as now we pray. _____

Apple-Red Happiness

Words and Music by
WARREN WATKINS

Ap - ple - red hap - pi - ness, Pop - corn cheer - ful - ness, Cin - na - mon sing - ing in - side; Pep - per - mint en - er - gy, Gum - drop hol - i - days When you give Christ your life! The ben - e - fits of God's great love Are su - per - sat - is - fy - ing. Throw a - way your sin!

My God Is So Big

97

Everything That Is, Is His

KATHIE HILL

DAVID HAMPTON

Ev - ery-thing that is, is His; All that's un - der and be - side us, The Fa - ther has sup - plied us.

God's still the own - er; He's just loan - ing it, you see, 'Cause

last time to Coda

ev - ery-thing that is, is His!

99 All Night, All Day

Spiritual
Arr. by Lyndell Leatherman

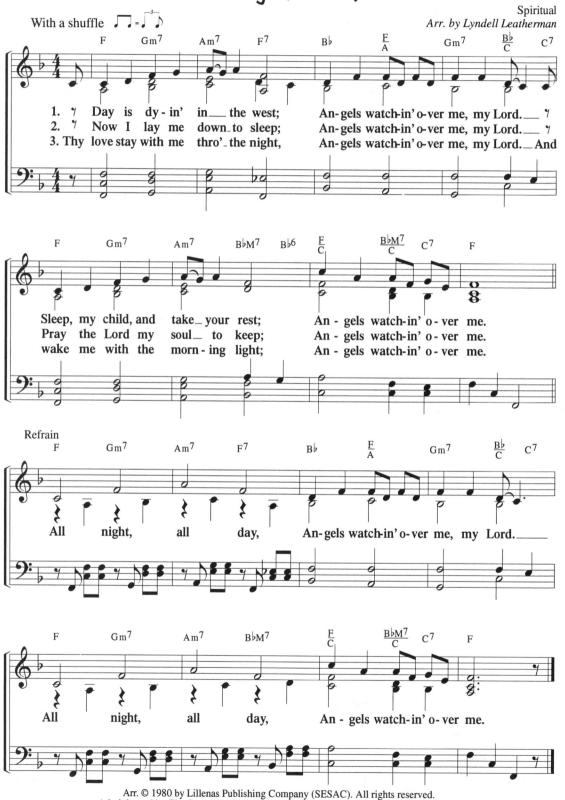

1. Day is dy-in' in the west;
   An-gels watch-in' o-ver me, my Lord.
2. Now I lay me down to sleep;
   An-gels watch-in' o-ver me, my Lord.
3. Thy love stay with me thro' the night,
   An-gels watch-in' o-ver me, my Lord. And

Sleep, my child, and take your rest;
   An-gels watch-in' o-ver me.
Pray the Lord my soul to keep;
   An-gels watch-in' o-ver me.
wake me with the morn-ing light;
   An-gels watch-in' o-ver me.

Refrain

All night, all day,
An-gels watch-in' o-ver me, my Lord.

All night, all day,
An-gels watch-in' o-ver me.

He's Got the Whole World in His Hands

Spiritual
Arr. by Lyndell Leatherman

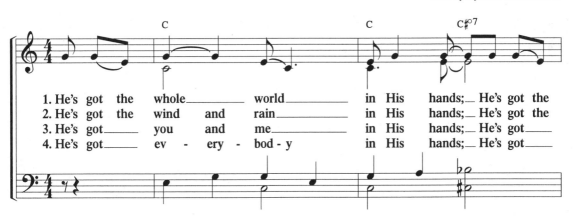

1. He's got the whole_____ world_____ in His hands;__ He's got the
2. He's got the wind and rain_____ in His hands;__ He's got the
3. He's got_____ you and me_____ in His hands;__ He's got
4. He's got_____ ev - ery - bod - y in His hands;__ He's got

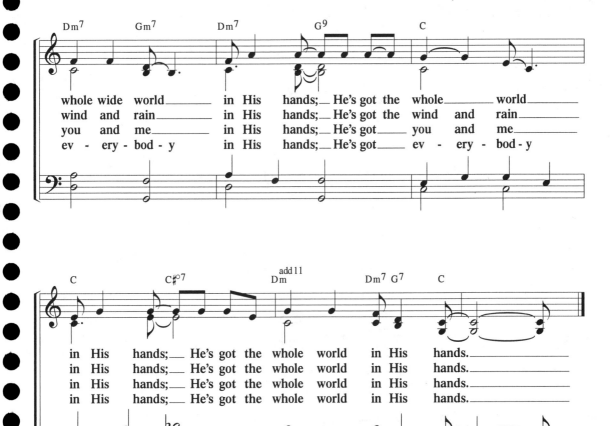

whole wide world_____ in His hands;__ He's got the whole_____ world_____
wind and rain_____ in His hands;__ He's got the wind and rain_____
you and me_____ in His hands;__ He's got_____ you and me_____
ev - ery - bod - y in His hands;__ He's got_____ ev - ery - bod - y

in His hands;__ He's got the whole world in His hands._____
in His hands;__ He's got the whole world in His hands._____
in His hands;__ He's got the whole world in His hands._____
in His hands;__ He's got the whole world in His hands._____

101

I Am a "C"

Unknown
Arr. by Lyndell Leatherman

I am a C, I am a C-H, I am a C-H-R-I-S-T-I-A-N; And I have C-H-R-I-S-T in my H-E-A-R-T and I will L-I-V-E E-T-E-R-N-A-L-L-Y.

*May be repeated several times, with gradually increasing speed.
Arr. © 1980 by Lillenas Publishing Company (SESAC). All rights reserved.
Administered by The Copyright Company, 40 Music Square East, Nashville, TN 37203.

102

Coming Again

Words and Music by
MOSIE LISTER

1. Je - sus is com - ing; Je - sus is com - ing;
2. In clouds of glo - ry, In clouds of glo - ry,
3. We'll rise to meet Him; We'll rise to meet Him;
4. We shall be like Him; We shall be like Him;
5. Oh, hal - le - lu - jah! Oh, hal - le - lu - jah!

Copyright © 1974 by Lillenas Publishing Company (SESAC). All rights reserved.
Administered by The Copyright Company, 40 Music Square East, Nashville, TN 37203.

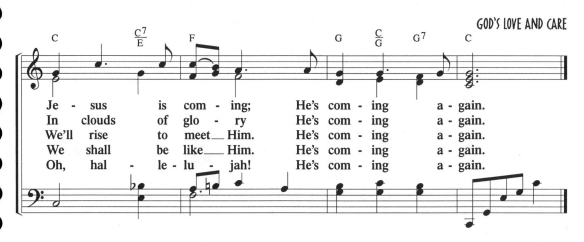

Je - sus is com - ing; He's com - ing a - gain.
In clouds of glo - ry He's com - ing a - gain.
We'll rise to meet Him. He's com - ing a - gain.
We shall be like Him. He's com - ing a - gain.
Oh, hal - le - lu - jah! He's com - ing a - gain.

Be Strong 103

KEN BIBLE

Traditional
Arr. by Lyndell Leatherman

1. Be strong and cou - ra - geous and bold; Be
2. He's with you wher - ev - er you go; He's
3. So trust Him with all of your heart; So

strong and cou - ra - geous and bold. A - way with your fear, for
with you wher - ev - er you go. He's there by your side to
trust Him with all of your heart. Be - lieve and o - bey each

God will be near. Be strong and cou - ra - geous and bold.
help and to guide. He's with you wher - ev - er you go.
hour of the day, And trust Him with all of your heart.

104

Jesus Loves Me

ANNA B. WARNER

WILLIAM B. BRADBURY

1. Je - sus loves me! this I know, For the Bi - ble tells me so.
2. Je - sus loves me! He who died Heav - en's gates to o - pen wide.

Lit - tle ones to Him be - long; They are weak, but He is strong.
He will wash a - way my sin, Let His lit - tle child come in.

Yes, Je - sus loves me. Yes, Je - sus loves me.

Yes, Je - sus loves me. The Bi - ble tells me so.

Enough Love

LINDA REBUCK

TOM FETTKE

God has e-nough love to go a-round;_____ Our God has e-nough love to share._____ All o-ver the world His chil-dren are found Re-ceiv-ing His love and His care._____

A-B-C-D-E-F-G

Words and Music by
HUBERT MITCHELL

When He Came

Words and Music by
MOSIE LISTER

1. He brought joy to the world when He came.
2. He brought peace to the world when He came.
3. He brought love to the world when He came.
4. He brought hope to the world when He came.

He brought joy to the world when He came.
He brought peace to the world when He came.
He brought love to the world when He came.
He brought hope to the world when He came.

To the hearts heav-y-bur-dened With trou-ble and with
To the man-y and the few, And e-ven me and
Love that lives be-yond the grave, My soul and yours to
To the rich man, to the poor man, The beg-gar, and the

strife, He brought joy, great joy when He came.
you, He brought peace, last-ing peace when He came.
save, He brought love, won-drous love when He came.
king, He brought hope, liv-ing hope when He came.

108 He'll Be Comin' Down from Heaven

DOUG JOHNSON, age 9

Traditional
Arr. by Lyndell Leatherman

In My Father's House

Traditional

*1. Come and go with me to my Fa-ther's house, To my Fa-ther's house,
2. It's not ver - y far to my Fa-ther's house, To my Fa-ther's house,
*3. Je - sus is the way to my Fa-ther's house, To my Fa-ther's house,

to my Fa-ther's house. Come and go with me to my Fa-ther's
to my Fa-ther's house. It's not ver - y far to my Fa-ther's
to my Fa-ther's house. Je - sus is the way to my Fa-ther's

house, Where there's joy, joy, joy.
house, Where there's joy, joy, joy.
house, Where there's joy, joy, joy.

joy, joy, joy, joy.

Optional verses:
4. Jesus is the Light in my Father's house . . .
5. All is peace and love in my Father's house . . .
6. We shall praise the Lord in my Father's house . . .

*Verses 1 and 3 on recording (with optional final ending).

A Great Big God

Words and Music by
MARK PENDERGRASS

1. You hung all the stars and
2. You con-trol the thun - der,

named them one by one;
cause the wind to blow,

You rolled out the moon and
Send the driv - ing rain and

lit the sun.
si - lent snow;

Tip-ping up the moun - tains,
O - pen ev - ery flow - er,

pour-ing out the sea;
col - or ev - ery tree;

Then You turned a - round and
Then You sit right down and

You made me.
talk to me.

There Were Twelve Disciples

Anonymous

GEORGE A. MINOR

There were twelve dis - ci - ples Je - sus called to help Him: Si - mon Pe - ter, An - drew,

James, his broth-er John; Phil - ip, Thom- as, Mat - thew, James, the son of Al - pheus,

Thad-deus, Si- mon, Ju - das, and Bar-thol-o - mew. He has called us, too; He has called us,

too. We are His dis-ci - ples; I am one, and you. We His work must do.

112
Only a Boy Named David

THE WRIGHT SINGERS

ARTHUR ARNOTT

Motions:
1. Hand held out as if measuring.
2. Wind arm as if preparing to throw ball underhanded.
3. Hands folded.
4. Arms extended, make fingers move imitating rippling of water.
5. Hold up five fingers.
6. Imitate putting stone in sling.
7. Release winding of arm as if stone is thrown.
8. Drop down.

Adam, Adam

Words and Music by
RHETT PARRISH, JODI HANNA, and ED KEE
Arr. by Ed Kee

*1. A - dam, A - dam, won't you tell us:
*2. No - ah, No - ah, won't you tell us:
3. Mo - ses, Mo - ses, won't you tell us:

How did you like par - a - dise? "God pro - vid - ed all I need - ed;
How'd you ev - er build that boat? "God pro - vid - ed all I need - ed;
How'd you ev - er part the seas? "God pro - vid - ed all I need - ed;

While it last - ed it was nice!"
Thro' the storm I stayed a - float."
With His help it was a breeze."

*4. Da - vid, Da - vid, won't you tell us: How'd you kill that Phil - is - tine?
5. Shad - rach, Shad - rach, won't you tell us: How did you es - cape those flames?

"God pro - vid - ed all I need - ed; With five peb - bles and a sling."
"God pro - vid - ed all I need - ed; All I did was call His name."

*Verses 1, 2, 4, 6, 8 on recording.

114 Shadrach, Meshach, and Abednego

Words and Music by
HUGH MITCHELL
Arr. by John W. Peterson

Three good men lived ver-y long a-go— Shad-rach, Me-shach, and A-bed-ni-go. To an i-dol they would nev-er bow— Shad-rach, Me-shach, and A-bed-ni-go. To a fi-ery fur-nace they were there-fore cast; Neb-u-chad-nez-zar thought they'd nev-er last. But God was there; He'd

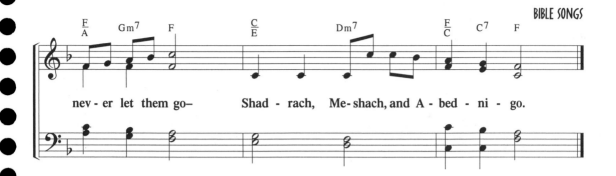

nev - er let them go— Shad - rach, Me - shach, and A - bed - ni - go.

Peter, James, and John in a Sailboat 115

Traditional
Arr. by Lyndell Leatherman

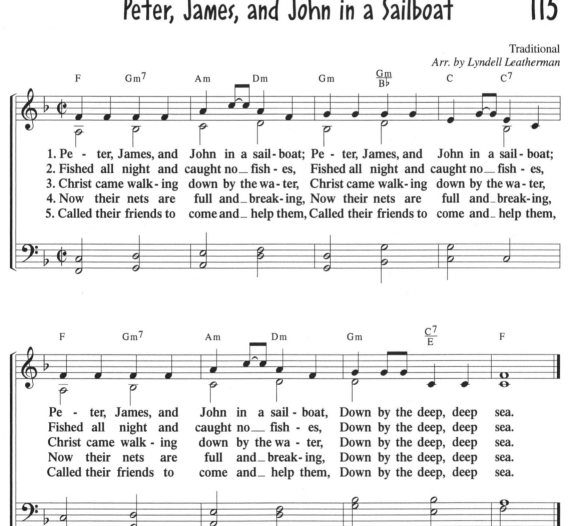

1. Pe - ter, James, and John in a sail - boat; Pe - ter, James, and John in a sail - boat;
2. Fished all night and caught no fish - es, Fished all night and caught no fish - es,
3. Christ came walk - ing down by the wa - ter, Christ came walk - ing down by the wa - ter,
4. Now their nets are full and break - ing, Now their nets are full and break - ing,
5. Called their friends to come and help them, Called their friends to come and help them,

Pe - ter, James, and John in a sail - boat, Down by the deep, deep sea.
Fished all night and caught no fish - es, Down by the deep, deep sea.
Christ came walk - ing down by the wa - ter, Down by the deep, deep sea.
Now their nets are full and break - ing, Down by the deep, deep sea.
Called their friends to come and help them, Down by the deep, deep sea.

Option: Arrange chairs in the shape of a boat; children sit in the middle.
    vs. 1: Sing only.
    vs. 2: Pretend to be fishing.
    vs. 3: Appoint "Christ" to walk around the "boat."
    vs. 4: Struggle with heavy nets.
    vs. 5: Cup hands to mouth as though calling.

Get in the Ark!

Words and Music by
SUZANNE H. CLASON

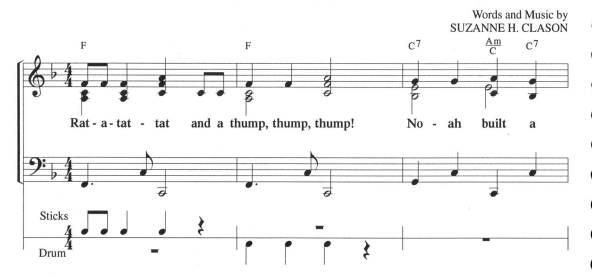

Rat - a - tat - tat and a thump, thump, thump! No - ah built a

Sticks

Drum

great big ark. Rat - a - tat - tat and a thump, thump, thump! For his

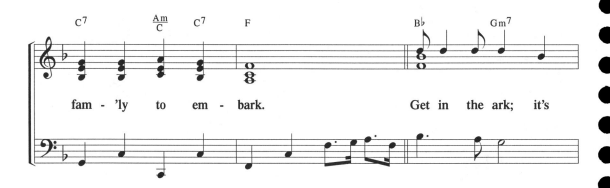

fam - 'ly to em - bark. Get in the ark; it's

go-ing to rain. *Here come the cows: "moo, moo, moo."

Get in the ark; it's go-ing to rain. Here come the an-i-mals two by two.

*Option: add other verses of animal sounds, but retain sounds of animals already in the ark. For example:

2. Here come the ducks: "quack, quack, quack," "moo, moo, moo"
3. Here come the pigs: "oink, oink, oink," "quack, quack, quack," etc.

Jesus Is Living in Heaven Today 117

MARGARET M. SELF   JEANNE P. LAWLER

1. Je - sus is liv-ing in heav-en to - day. How do I know? How do I know?
2. All who love Je-sus will see Him some-day. How do I know? How do I know?
3. We will be hap-py in heav-en some-day. How do I know? How do I know?
4. Je-sus has prom-ised He will come a - gain. How do I know? How do I know?

Je-sus is liv-ing in heav-en to-day: The Bi-ble tells me so.
All who love Je-sus will see Him some-day: The Bi-ble tells me so.
We will be hap-py in heav-en some-day: The Bi-ble tells me so.
Je-sus has prom-ised He will come a - gain: The Bi-ble tells me so.

118 The Wise Man and the Foolish Man

Adapted from Scripture

Unknown

rains came down and the floods came up, And the house on the rock stood fast.
And the house on the sand went smash.

The B-I-B-L-E

119

DWIGHT UPHAUS   Traditional

1. The B - I - B - L - E,   It is God's
2. The B - I - B - L - E,   Yes, it's the
3. The B - I - B - L - E,   Its sto - ries

Word to me.   I will o - bey God's
book for me.   I love to hear the
help me see   The love of Je - sus,

Ho - ly Word, The B - I - B - L - E.
sto - ries from The B - I - B - L - E.
God's own Son; The B - I - B - L - E.

120

Arky, Arky

Traditional

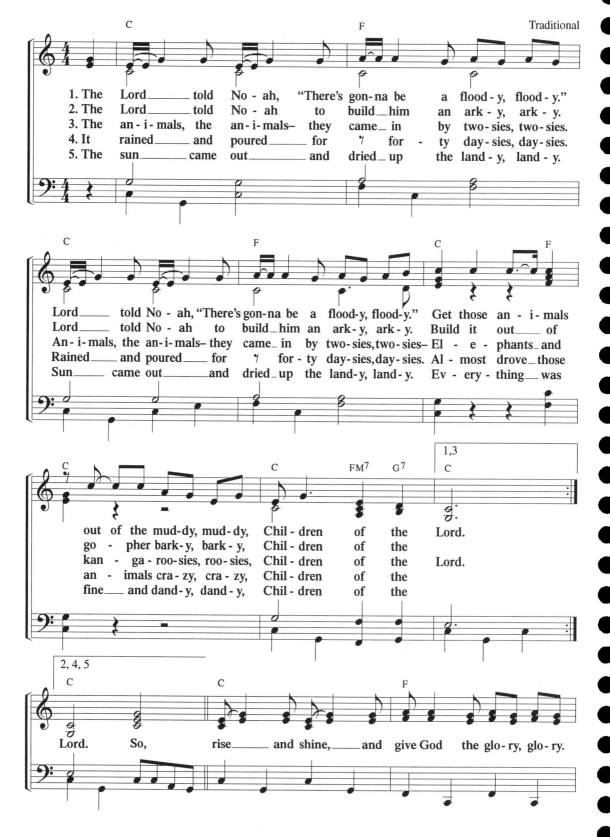

1. The Lord told No - ah, "There's gon-na be a flood-y, flood-y."
2. The Lord told No - ah to build him an ark-y, ark-y.
3. The an - i- mals, the an - i- mals– they came in by two-sies, two-sies.
4. It rained and poured for 'r for - ty day-sies, day-sies.
5. The sun came out and dried up the land-y, land-y.

Lord told No - ah, "There's gon-na be a flood-y, flood-y." Get those an - i- mals
Lord told No - ah to build him an ark-y, ark-y. Build it out of
An - i- mals, the an - i- mals– they came in by two-sies, two-sies– El - e - phants and
Rained and poured for 'r for - ty day-sies, day-sies. Al - most drove those
Sun came out and dried up the land-y, land-y. Ev - ery - thing was

1,3

out of the mud-dy, mud-dy, Chil - dren of the Lord.
go - pher bark- y, bark- y, Chil - dren of the
kan - ga - roo-sies, roo-sies, Chil - dren of the Lord.
an - imals cra - zy, cra - zy, Chil - dren of the
fine and dand-y, dand-y, Chil - dren of the

2, 4, 5

Lord. So, rise and shine, and give God the glo-ry, glo-ry.

John 3:16

121

122

Hey, Jonah!

KEN BIBLE

WILLIAM B. BRADBURY

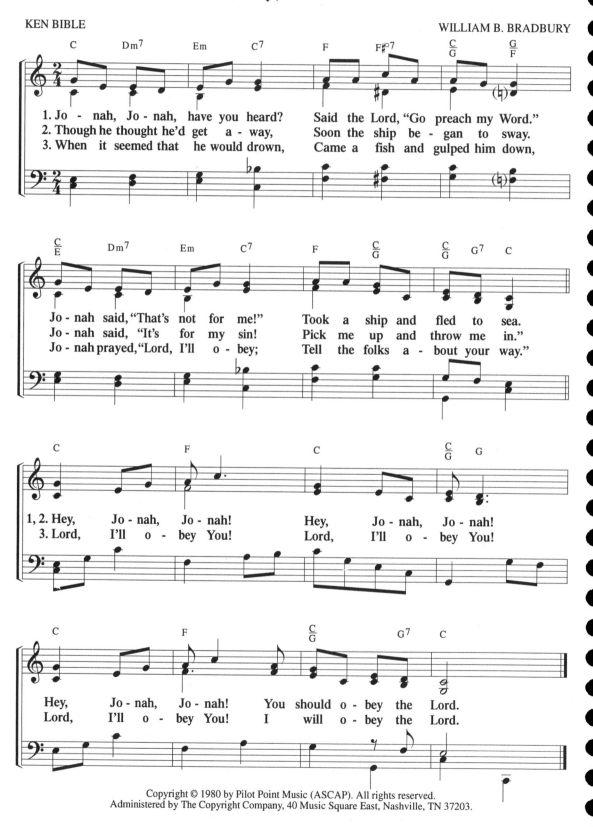

1. Jo - nah, Jo - nah, have you heard? Said the Lord, "Go preach my Word."
2. Though he thought he'd get a - way, Soon the ship be - gan to sway.
3. When it seemed that he would drown, Came a fish and gulped him down,

Jo - nah said, "That's not for me!" Took a ship and fled to sea.
Jo - nah said, "It's for my sin! Pick me up and throw me in."
Jo - nah prayed, "Lord, I'll o - bey; Tell the folks a - bout your way."

1, 2. Hey, Jo - nah, Jo - nah! Hey, Jo - nah, Jo - nah!
3. Lord, I'll o - bey You! Lord, I'll o - bey You!

Hey, Jo - nah, Jo - nah! You should o - bey the Lord.
Lord, I'll o - bey You! I will o - bey the Lord.

There's No One Exactly like Me

TRILBY JORDAN

BETTY ANN RAMSETH

1. Look all the world o - ver; there's no one like me,
2. Some peo - ple are short and some peo - ple are tall.
3. Some fac - es are dark and some fac - es are light.
4. Look all the world o - ver; there's no one like me,

No one like me,_____ no one like me. Look
God loves them all,_____ God loves them all. Some
Each one is spe - cial in God's lov - ing sight. Some
No one like me,_____ no one like me. Look

all the world o - ver, there's no one like me; There's
peo - ple are short and some peo - ple are tall, But
fac - es are dark and some fac - es are light, But
all the world o - ver, there's no one like me; There's

no one ex - act - ly like me._____
no one's ex - act - ly like me._____
no one's ex - act - ly like me._____
no one ex - act - ly like me._____

Kids Under Construction

GLORIA GAITHER
and GARY S. PAXTON

WILLIAM J. GAITHER and
GARY S. PAXTON

Kids under con-struc - tion—

May - be the paint is still wet.

Kids under con-struc - tion— The

Lord may not be fin - ished yet.

*Verses 1 and 3 on recording

125

I Am a Promise

WILLIAM J. GAITHER
and GLORIA GAITHER

WILLIAM J. GAITHER

I am a prom-ise, I am a pos-si-bil-i-ty; I am a prom-ise with a cap-i-tal "P".___ I am a great big bun-dle of po-ten-ti-al-i-ty.___ And I am learn-ing to hear God's voice,___ And I am try-ing to make the right choic-es. I'm a prom-ise to be___

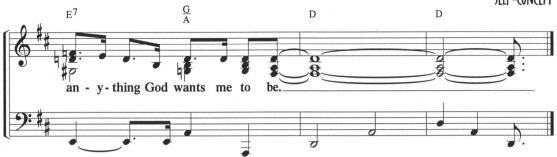

an - y - thing God wants me to be.

Jesus Loves Even Me

126

Words and Music by
PHILIP P. BLISS

I   am so glad that our   Fa - ther in heav'n   Tells of His love in the
Won - der-ful things in the   Bi - ble I   see;   This is the dear - est, that

Book He has giv'n.
Je - sus loves me.   I am so glad   that Je - sus loves me,

Je - sus loves me,   Je - sus loves me.   Je - sus loves e - ven me!

The Butterfly Song

Words and Music by
BRIAN HOWARD

1. If I were a but-ter-fly,_____ I'd thank You, Lord, for giv-ing me wings. And if I were a rob-in in a tree, I'd thank you, Lord, that I could sing. And if I were a fish in the sea,_____ I'd
2. If I were an el-e-phant,_____ I'd thank You, Lord, by rais-ing my trunk. And if I were a kan-ga-roo, You know I'd hop right up to You. And if I were an oc-to-pus,_____ I'd
3. If I were a wig-gly worm,_____ I'd thank You, Lord, that I____ could squirm. And if I were a bil-ly____ goat, I'd thank You, Lord, for my strong throat. And if I were a fuz-zy-wuz-zy bear, I'd

128
I'm Something Special

WILLIAM J. and GLORIA GAITHER

WILLIAM J. GAITHER

Boys 1. I have a lit-tle sis-ter who's not at all like me; She can

Girls 2. My dad-dy mows the back yard; my moth-er makes the bed; My

write a love-ly po-em, but I can climb a tree. My

broth-er cleans the play-room; I see the dog gets fed. And

broth-er too is dif-f'rent, with freck-les on his nose; When my

each one needs the oth-er to help him through the day; And

ques-tions need-ed an-swers, he's the one who knows.

love must be the rea-son God planned it just that way.

Sandy Land

Words and Music by
KAREN LAFFERTY

Don't build your house on the sand-y land,___ Don't build it too near the shore.___

Well, it might look kind of nice, But you'll have to build it twice; Oh, you'll have to build your

house once more. more. You bet-ter build your house up-on a rock, Make a

good foun-da-tion on a sol-id spot.___ Oh, the storms may come and go,___

But the peace of God you will know. more. Well, it might look kind of

nice, But you'll have to build it twice; Oh, you'll have to build your house once more.

I Have Decided to Follow Jesus 130

Traditional

1. I have de - cid - ed_____ to fol - low Je - sus;_____ I have de -
2. The world be - hind me,_____ the cross be - fore me;_____ The world be -
3. Tho' none go with me,_____ still I will fol - low;_____ Tho' none go
4. Will you de - cide now_____ to fol - low Je - sus?_____ Will you de -

cid - ed_____ to fol - low Je - sus;_____ I have de - cid - ed_____ to fol - low
hind me,_____ the cross be - fore me;_____ The world be - hind me,_____ the cross be -
with me,_____ still I will fol - low;_____ Tho' none go with me,_____ still I will
cide now_____ to fol - low Je - sus?_____ Will you de - cide now_____ to fol - low

Je - sus;_____ No turn - ing back,_____ no turn - ing back._____
fore me;_____ No turn - ing back,_____ no turn - ing back._____
fol - low;_____ No turn - ing back,_____ no turn - ing back._____
Je - sus?_____ No turn - ing back,_____ no turn - ing back._____

Fishers of Men

Words and Music by
HARRY D. CLARKE

1. I will make you fish-ers of men, Fish-ers of men, fish-ers of men. I will make you fish-ers of men if you fol - low Me. If you fol - low Me, if you fol - low Me, I will make you fish-ers of men if you fol - low Me.

2. Hear Christ call - ing, "Come un-to Me, Come un-to Me, come un-to Me." Hear Christ call - ing, "Come un-to Me; I will give you rest. I will give you rest." Hear Christ call - ing, "Come un-to Me; I will give you rest."

My Hands Belong to You

132

Words and Music by
ANE WEBER and
FRANK HERNANDEZ

1. My hands be-long to You, Lord; My hands be-long to You. I lift them up to You, Lord, And sing hal-le-lu-jah. I lift them up to You, Lord, And sing hal-le-lu-jah.

2. My voice be-longs to You, Lord; My voice be-longs to You. I lift it up to You, Lord, And sing hal-le-lu-jah. I lift it up to You, Lord, And sing hal-le-lu-jah.

3. My heart be-longs to You, Lord; My heart be-longs to You. I lift it up to You, Lord, And sing hal-le-lu-jah. I lift it up to You, Lord, And sing hal-le-lu-jah.

We Are the Light

Words and Music by
TOM MCLAIN

⊕ CODA

Al - le - lu - ia!___ We are the light of the world.___

Al - le - lu - ia!___ We are the light of the world.

We are the light of the world;___

We are the salt of the earth.___ We are to spread the light;

We are to do what's right. We are the light of the world.___

8vb

Seek Ye First

Words and Music by
KAREN LAFFERTY

Stop, Go, Watch

Unknown

*1. Stop, and let me tell you what the Lord has done for me.
*2. Go, and tell the sto - ry of the Christ of Cal - va - ry.
3. Watch, and be ye read - y, for the Lord may come to - day.

Stop, and let me tell you what the Lord has done for me. He for-
Go, and tell the sto - ry of the Christ of Cal - va - ry. He'll for-
Watch, and be ye read - y, for the Lord may come to - day. He will

gave my sin and He saved my soul,— He cleansed my heart and He made me whole.
give their sins, He will save their souls;— He'll cleanse their hearts, He will make them whole.
come a - gain in the clouds for me— And take me home for e - ter - ni - ty.

Stop, and let me tell you what the Lord has done for me.
Go, and tell the sto - ry of the Christ of Cal - va - ry.
Watch, and be ye read - y, for the Lord may come to - day.

*Verses 1 and 2 on recording.

136

Love Is Patient

LYNNE BROWER and CAROL McMILLEN

Traditional

Love is pa-tient, love is pa-tient, Love is kind, love is kind; Al-ways un-der-stand-ing, al-ways un-der-stand-ing Time af-ter time, time af-ter time.

137

I Wonder How It Felt

WILLIAM J. GAITHER
and GLORIA GAITHER

WILLIAM J. GAITHER

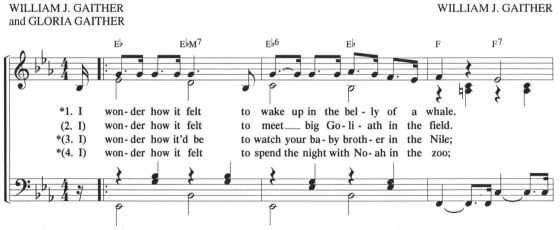

*1. I won-der how it felt to wake up in the bel-ly of a whale.
(2. I) won-der how it felt to meet___ big Go-li-ath in the field.
*(3. I) won-der how it'd be to watch your ba-by broth-er in the Nile;
*(4. I) won-der how it felt to spend the night with No-ah in the zoo;

*Verses 1, 3-4 on recording.

I won-der how it felt   to spend the night with Si-las in the jail.
I won-der how it felt   to know the mouths of li-ons have been sealed.
I won-der who would come,   a prin-cess or a hun-gry croc-o-dile.
I won-der how it felt   to sleep be-side a smell-y kan-ga-roo.

I'm   just a child;   my   life is still be-fore me.   I   just can't

wait   to   see what God has for   me. But   I   know that I   will trust Him, And I'll

wait   to   see   what life   will   be   for   me.

2. I
3. I   me.
4. I

We Are the Children

Words and Music by
TOM MCLAIN

We are the chil - dren of __ the King. __ We want to laugh __ and we want __ to sing. __ We want to share __ the joy - ful news __ That Je - sus Christ __ is call - ing you.

Fine 3rd time

1. All o - ver the world, _____ the
2. We are __ His own; _____ He has

mes - age is the same: _____ He died __ for you,
bought us with a price– _____ His pre - cious blood,

and then He rose a - gain.
and He's called us to His light.

God Calls Us

139

LINDA REBUCK

TOM FETTKE

*1. Be - cause so man - y need to know, It's up to
2. Be - cause so man - y need to see That God a -
*3. Be - cause so man - y need to hear, I want to

you and me to go. Be - cause so man - y need to
lone can make them free; Be - cause so man - y need to
be a vol - un - teer. Be - cause so man - y need to

know, God calls us, God calls us.
see, God calls us, God calls us.
hear, God calls us, God calls us.

*Verses 1 and 3 on recording.

140 Actions Speak Louder than Words

Words and Music by
KATHIE HILL

Teach Me, Lord

LINDA REBUCK

TOM FETTKE

142

Love, Love, Love

HERBERT BROKERING

LOIS BROKERING

1. Love, love, love! That's what it's all a-
2. Peace, peace, peace!
3. Joy, joy, joy!

bout! 'Cause God loves us, we love each oth - er.

Moth - er, fa - ther, sis - ter, broth - er. Ev - ery-bod-y sing and

shout 'Cause that's what it's all a - bout!

1. It's a-bout
2. It's a-bout
3. It's a-bout

love, love, love; It's a-bout love, love, love!
peace, peace, peace; It's a-bout peace, peace, peace!
joy, joy, joy; It's a-bout joy, joy, joy!

Into My Heart

143

Words and Music by
HARRY D. CLARKE

In - to my heart, in - to my heart, Come in - to my

heart, Lord Je - sus. Come in to - day, come

in to stay; Come in - to my heart, Lord Je - sus.

144

Philippians 4:13

Words and Music by
HOMER W. GRIMES

I can do all things thro' Christ who strength-en-eth me.

I can do all things thro' Christ who strength-en-eth me.

Day by day, hour by hour, I am kept by His pow'r.

I can do all things thro' Christ who strength-en-eth me.

O How He Loves You and Me

Words and Music by
KURT KAISER

146

We Have a King

FRED KAAN

Traditional

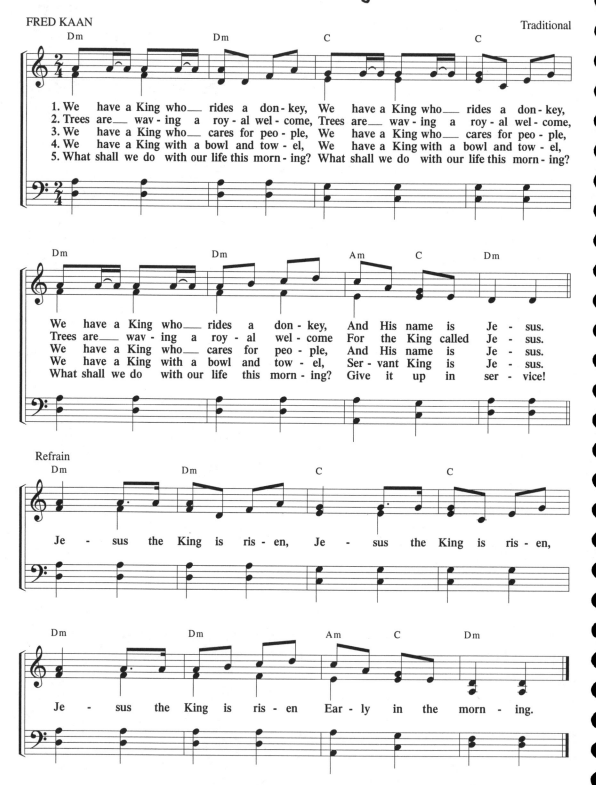

1. We have a King who rides a don-key, We have a King who rides a don-key,
2. Trees are wav-ing a roy-al wel-come, Trees are wav-ing a roy-al wel-come,
3. We have a King who cares for peo-ple, We have a King who cares for peo-ple,
4. We have a King with a bowl and tow-el, We have a King with a bowl and tow-el,
5. What shall we do with our life this morn-ing? What shall we do with our life this morn-ing?

We have a King who rides a don-key, And His name is Je-sus.
Trees are wav-ing a roy-al wel-come For the King called Je-sus.
We have a King who cares for peo-ple, And His name is Je-sus.
We have a King with a bowl and tow-el, Ser-vant King is Je-sus.
What shall we do with our life this morn-ing? Give it up in ser-vice!

Refrain

Je - sus the King is ris - en, Je - sus the King is ris - en,

Je - sus the King is ris - en Ear - ly in the morn - ing.

Bethlehem Lullaby

P. W. BLACKNER

JOHANNES BRAHMS
Arr. by Lyndell Leatherman

1. Long a - go there was born In the cit - y of Da - vid A sweet ho - ly Babe Who was Je - sus, our King. An - gels sang at His birth, "Lul - la - by, peace on earth." An - gels sang at His birth, "Lul - la - by, peace on earth."

2. Je - sus came as a child From His Fa - ther in heav - en, And has shown us the way To be lov - ing and kind; While the stars sang a - bove, "Lul - la - by, God is love." While the stars sang a - bove, "Lul - la - by, God is love."

Amen!

Traditional

Traditional Spiritual
Arr. by Lyndell Leatherman

*Verses 1-3, 5-6 on recording.

Just a lit - tle ba - by.
Talk - in' to the el - ders.
Preach - in' 'bout the king - dom.
Bowed in deep - est sor - row,
Dy - ing for our sins,_____
Ris - en from the dead._____
And His name is Je - sus.
   Sing it o - ver,

Hear the an - gels sing - ing!
Mar - vel at His wis - dom!
Mir - a - cles and won - ders!
Pray - ing to His Fa - ther!
Lov - ing and for - giv - ing!
He will live for - ev - er!
Glo - ry, hal - le - lu - jah!
Glo - ry, hal - le - lu - jah!

a - men!_____

(last time only)

A - men, a -

A - men, a - men, a -

1-7

8   great rit.

men, a - men!

men, a - men!

Come On, Ring Those Bells

Words and Music by
ANDREW CULVERWELL

1. Ev-ery-bod-y likes to take a hol-i-day;
2. Cel-e-bra-tions come be-cause of some-thing good,

Ev-ery-bod-y likes to take a rest,   Spend-ing time to-
Cel-e-bra-tions we love to re-call.   Mar-y had a

geth-er with the fam-i-ly,____ Shar-ing lots of love and hap-pi-
ba-by boy in Beth-le-hem,____ The great-est cel-e-bra-tion of them

Refrain

ness.
all.   Come on, ring those bells;   light the Christ-mas

tree.   Je-sus is the King   born for you and me.

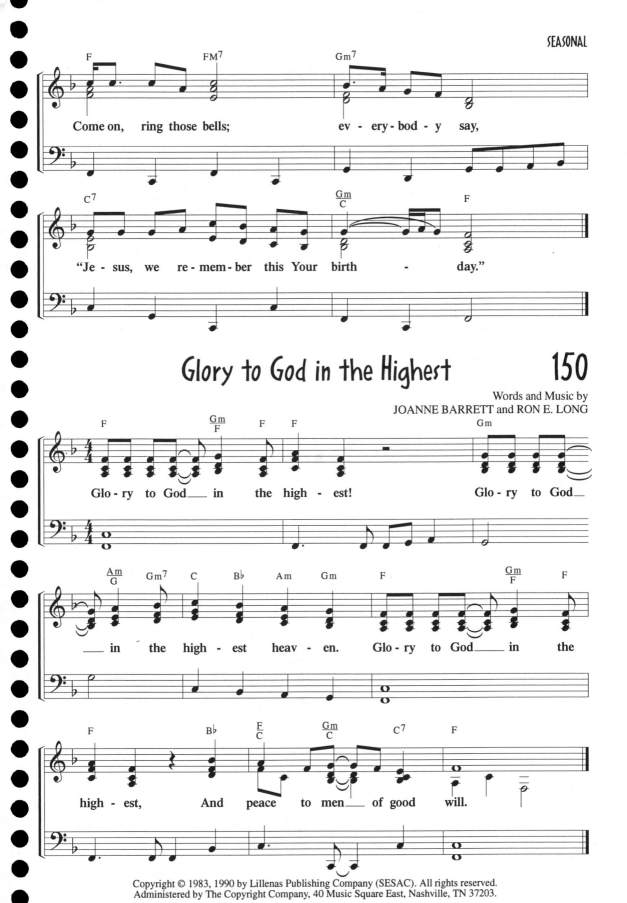

Come on, ring those bells; ev - ery - bod - y say, "Je - sus, we re - mem - ber this Your birth - day."

Glory to God in the Highest 150

Words and Music by
JOANNE BARRETT and RON E. LONG

Glo - ry to God in the high - est! Glo - ry to God in the high - est heav - en. Glo - ry to God in the high - est, And peace to men of good will.

151 Go, Tell It on the Mountain

JOHN W. WORK, JR.   Afro-American Spiritual

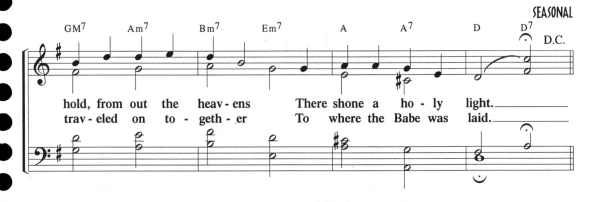

GM⁷ | Am⁷ | Bm⁷ | Em⁷ | A | A⁷ | D | D⁷ D.C.

hold, from out the heav - ens   There shone a ho - ly light._____
trav - eled on to - geth - er   To where the Babe was laid._____

Immanuel, Immanuel

152

Words and Music by
DAN WHITTEMORE

Im - man - u - el, Im - man - u - el, God is with us, Im - man - u -

el. They shall call Him Im - man - u - el, God is with__ us.

Im - man - u -   God is with__ us.__

Jesus Is His Name

Words and Music by
PAUL and DONNA WILLIAMS

1. There is a king who was born in a man-ger; Je-sus was His name.
   Came to__ earth, to His own was a strang-er;
   Je - sus is His name.__

2. Sheep are__ graz-ing__ on the__ hill - side; Shep - herds watch their flock.
   An - gels__ sing, "The__ King is__ born;
   Je - sus is His name."__

3. Shep - herds come to__ see the__ Child; Je - sus is His name.
   Lamb of__ God, so__ meek and__ mild;
   Je - sus is His name.__

Refrain

Al - le-lu - ia! Al - le-lu - ia! Hear the an-gels sing.

King of Kings and Lord__ of Lords! Je - sus is His name.__

Holy Ground

Words and Music by
GERON DAVIS
Arr. by Joseph Linn

CELEBRATION MEDLEY

"Sing, Shout, Clap" 1 time, repeating as directed. "He Is the King" 2 times, with optional tag

155

Sing, Shout, Clap

Words and Music by
BILLY FUNK
Arr. by Joseph Linn

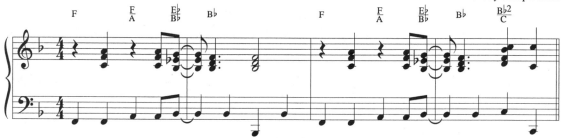

Sing, shout, clap—your hands; give praise un-to your Mak-er.——

Make a joy-ful noise—— un-to the Lord.——

Sing, shout, clap—your hands; give praise un-to your Mak-er, For the Lord—

name._____ For the Lord–

_____ He is Al - might-y God._____ For the Lord–

_____ He is Al - might-y God._____

156

He Is the King of Kings

Words and Music by
VIRGIL MEARES
Arr. by Joseph Linn

157 Holy, Holy, Holy! Lord God Almighty

REGINALD HEBER

JOHN B. DYKES
Arr. by Joseph Linn

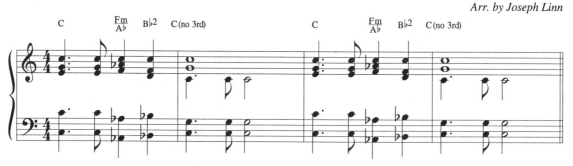

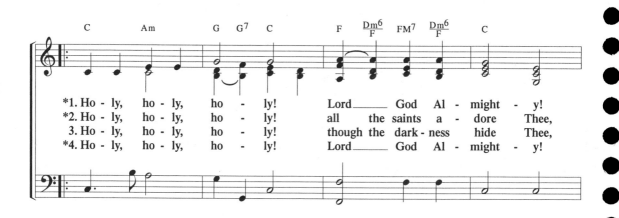

*1. Ho - ly, ho - ly, ho - ly! Lord_____ God Al - might - y!
*2. Ho - ly, ho - ly, ho - ly! all the saints a - dore Thee,
3. Ho - ly, ho - ly, ho - ly! though the dark - ness hide Thee,
*4. Ho - ly, ho - ly, ho - ly! Lord_____ God Al - might - y!

Ear - ly in the morn - ing our song shall rise to Thee.
Cast - ing down their gold - en crowns a - round the glass - y sea.
Though the eye of sin - ful man Thy glo - ry may not see.
All Thy works shall praise Thy name in earth and sky and sea.

*Verses 1, 2, and 4 on recording.

MIGHTY GOD MEDLEY

"What a Mighty God We Serve" 2 times, medley ending 2nd time. "How Great, How Glorious" 1 time, using all repeats

158 What a Mighty God We Serve

Unknown
Arr. by Joseph Linn

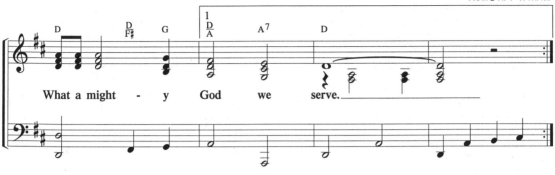

What a might - y God we serve.

2 Song ending

God we serve.

2 Medley ending   Driving ♩ = ca. 144

God we serve.

How Great, How Glorious

159

Words and Music by
MARTIN J. NYSTROM
and DON MOEN
Arr. by Joseph Linn

Driving ♩ = ca. 144

How great, how glo - ri - ous,___ how won - drous are_ Your ways;___ You reign vic - to - ri - ous,___ lift - ed

Isn't He?

Words and Music by
JOHN WIMBER
Arr. by Joseph Linn

Bless the Lord

Words and Music by
JOANNE BARRETT
and RON LONG

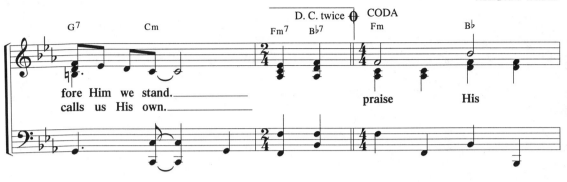

fore Him we stand.
calls us His own.

praise His

name.

Our New Song of Praise

162

Words and Music by
KEN BIBLE

A new song, a new song we

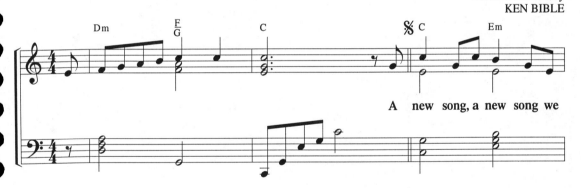

sing to the Lord. Our song is of praise, hal-le-lu-jah! He

HYMNS OF PRAISE MEDLEY

"All Creatures of Our God and King" both verses, medley ending 2nd time. "Joyful, Joyful, We Adore Thee" both verses, optional tag.

All Creatures of Our God and King

163

FRANCIS OF ASSISI, tr. by William H. Draper

Geistlich Kirchengesang
Arr. by Joseph Linn

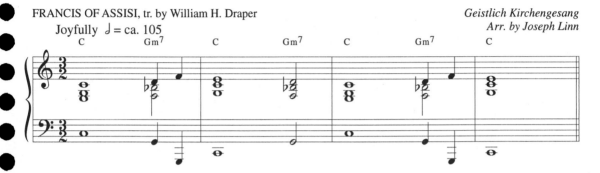

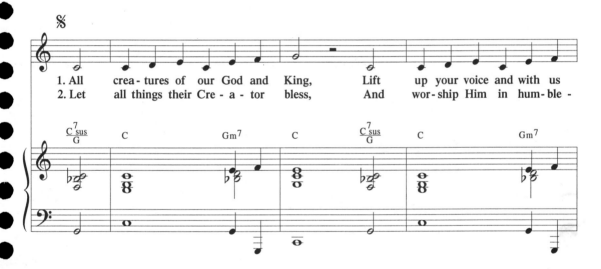

1. All crea-tures of our God and King, Lift up your voice and with us
2. Let all things their Cre-a-tor bless, And wor-ship Him in hum-ble-

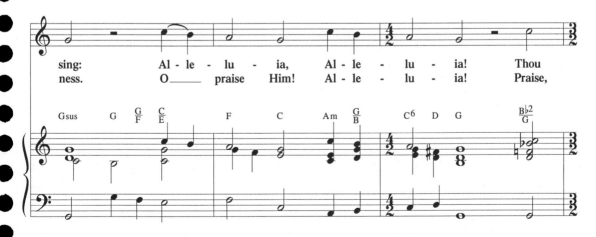

sing: Al-le-lu - ia, Al-le - lu - ia! Thou
ness. O___ praise Him! Al-le - lu - ia! Praise,

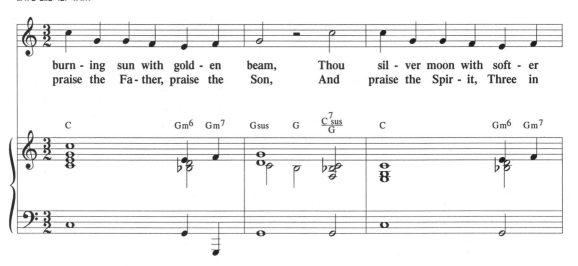

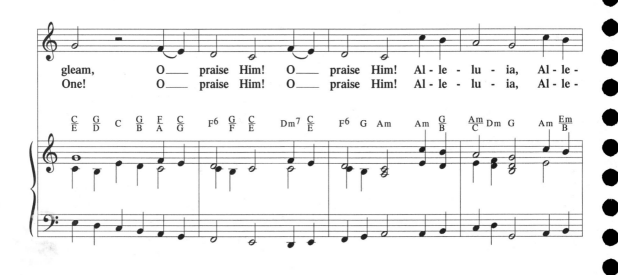

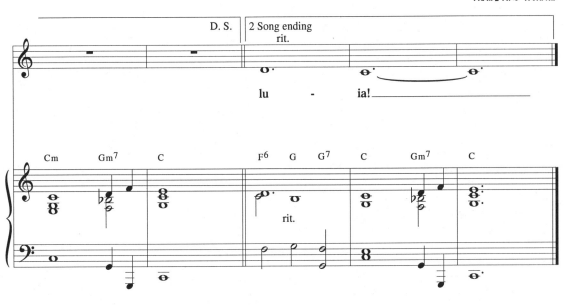

Joyful, Joyful, We Adore Thee

HENRY VAN DYKE

LUDWIG VAN BEETHOVEN
Arr. by Joseph Linn

Omit introduction if continuing from previous song.

1. Joy - ful, joy - ful, we a - dore Thee,
2. All Thy works with joy sur - round Thee,

God of glo - ry, Lord of love; Hearts un - fold like
Earth and heav'n re - flect Thy rays. Stars and an - gels

flow'rs be - fore Thee, Open - ing to the sun a - bove.
sing a - round Thee, Cen - ter of un - brok - en praise.

Melt the clouds of sin and sad - ness; Drive the dark of
Field and for - est, vale and moun - tain, Flow - ery mead - ow,

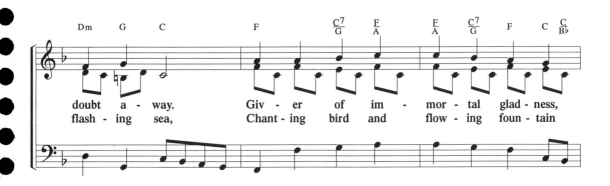

doubt a - way. Giv - er of im - mor - tal glad - ness,
flash - ing sea, Chant - ing bird and flow - ing foun - tain

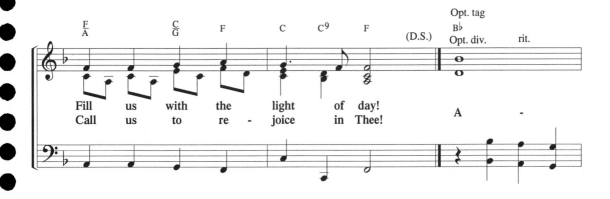

Fill us with the light of day!
Call us to re - joice in Thee! A -

men, a - men.

165 Nobody Else

LINDA REBUCK

TOM FETTKE

1. There was a time when this old earth was just an emp - ty
2. As time went by, man - kind be - came as sin - ful as could
3. Well, man - y years had come and gone since No - ah's float - ing

ball. God made the light, the birds and trees,_____ crea - tures large and
be. No one be - lieved in God at all but No - ah's fam - i -
zoo, And sin - ful man was still the same: God knew what He must

small. He filled the land with fire - flies, gi - raffes and aard - varks,
ly. So then the Lord said, "Take them all in - to a great big
do. He sent His Son in - to the world to die up - on a

too; And then He made a talk - ing thing that looks a lot like
boat." And plan - et Earth was wa - ter - logged, but No - ah stayed a -
tree, So ev - ery - one who trusts in Him will live e - ter - nal -

Gsus Gsus Gsus Gsus

you! _____
float! _____
ly. _____

Oh,

Refrain

F $\frac{C}{E}$ $\frac{G^7}{D}$ C

no-bod-y else could do that, No-bod-y else could do that–

F $\frac{C}{E}$ $\frac{E^7}{G\#}$ Am D^7

No one ex-cept the great "I AM"; _____ He

$\frac{C}{G}$ Gsus 1, 2 C $\frac{Dm^7}{C}$

must be the God of A - bra - ham.

D. C. 3

$\frac{G}{C}$ $\frac{F}{C}$ $\frac{F}{C}$ C C C

ham. _____

166 O Come, Let Us Adore Him

JOHN. F. WADE. and Unknown

JOHN F. WADE
Arr. by Joseph Linn

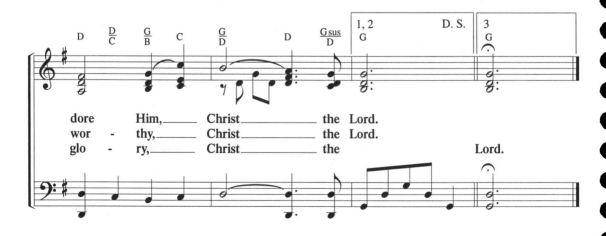

I WILL SING MEDLEY

"I Will Sing of the Mercies" 1 time. "I Will Call upon the Lord" 1 time, with repeats.

I Will Sing of the Mercies

167

Adapted from Psalm 89:1

Unknown

168

I Will Call upon the Lord

Words and Music by
MICHAEL O'SHIELDS

Opt. echo part (2nd time)

I will call up-on the Lord

I will call up-on the Lord   Who is wor-thy to_ be

Who is wor-thy to_ be praised;   So shall I be

praised;   So shall I be saved from my en - e - mies.___

saved from my en-e-mies.___ I will call up-on_ the

I will call up-on_ the Lord.

EMMANUEL MEDLEY

"Jesus, Name Above All Names" 2 times. "Emmanuel" 2 times.

169

Jesus, Name Above All Names

NAIDA HEARN   PATRICIA CAIN

Emmanuel

Words and Music by
BOB McGEE

Em - man - u - el,   Em - man - u - el,

His name   is called   Em - man - u - el; _____

_____ God   with us,   re - vealed in us,

Conclusion of medley

His name   is called   Em - man - u - el. _____

171

Hosanna

Words and Music by
CARL TUTTLE
Arr. by Joseph Linn

Triumphantly ♩ = ca. 102

1,3. Ho - san - na, ho - san - na, ho -
2. Glo - ry, glo - ry,

san-na in the high - est; Ho - san - na, ho -
glo - ry to the King of Kings! Glo - ry,

san - na, ho - san - na in the high - est;
glo - ry, glo - ry to the King of Kings!

BLESS HIS NAME MEDLEY

"Bless His Holy Name" 1 time. "Blessed Be the Lord" 1 time, both verses.

172 ## Bless His Holy Name

Words and Music by
ANDRAÉ CROUCH

Blessed Be the Lord

Words and Music by
KEN BIBLE

174 Great Is Thy Faithfulness

THOMAS O. CHISHOLM

WILLIAM M. RUNYAN

1. Great is Thy faith-ful-ness, O God, my Fa-ther;
2. Sum-mer and win-ter and spring-time and har-vest,

There is no shad-ow of turn-ing with Thee.
Sun, moon and stars in their cours-es a-bove

Thou chang-est not; Thy com-pas-sions, they fail not.
Join with all na-ture in man-i-fold wit-ness

As Thou hast been, Thou for-ev-er wilt be.
To Thy great faith-ful-ness, mer-cy and love.

He Is the Way

Words and Music by
OTIS SKILLINGS

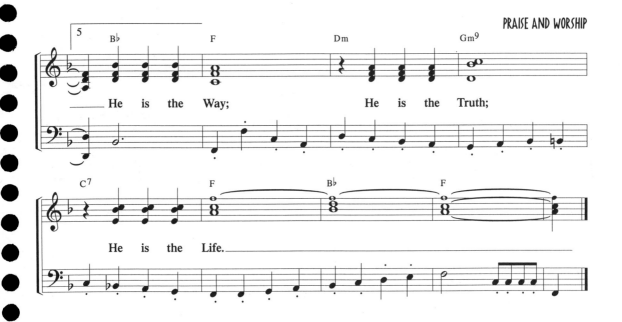

He is the Way; He is the Truth;

He is the Life.

Everybody Ought to Know

Traditional
Arr. by Lyndell Leatherman

Ev - ery - bod - y ought to know, Ev - ery - bod - y ought to know, Ev - ery - bod - y ought to

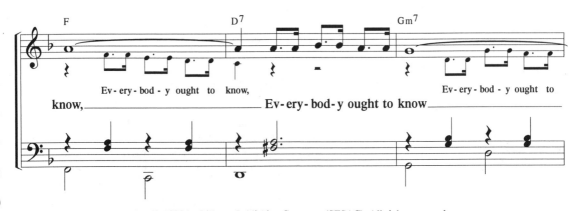

know, Ev - ery - bod - y ought to know Ev - ery - bod - y ought to know, Ev - ery - bod - y ought to

Sing and Celebrate

Words and Music by
CHARLES F. BROWN

Sing and cel - e - brate_ this day the Lord has made.

Sing and cel - e - brate_ the smile up - on your face.

Je - sus loves me! That's why I can say

I want to sing and cel - e - brate_ to - day.

PRAISED AND EXALTED MEDLEY

"I Will Sing Praise to the Name of Jesus" 2 times, medley ending 2nd time. "He Is Exalted" 2 times.

178 I Will Sing Praise to the Name of Jesus

Words and Music by
DAN WHITTEMORE
Arr. by Joseph Linn

He Is Exalted

Words and Music by
TWILA PARIS
Arr. by Joseph Linn

ev - er His truth shall reign. Heav - en and earth_____ re -

joice in His ho - ly name._____ He is ex- alt- ed, the King is ex- alt- ed on

high._____ high.

Conclusion of medley

He is ex- alt- ed, the King is ex- alt- ed on high._____

180

One Big Hallelujah

Words and Music by
CHRIS CHRISTENSEN
Arr. by Joseph Linn

Country feel ♩ = 92

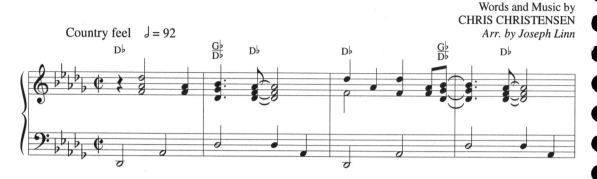

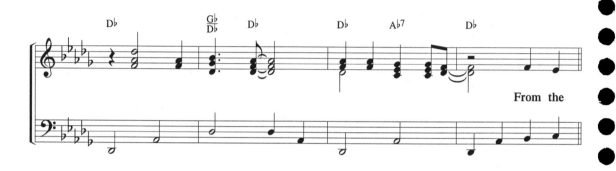

From the

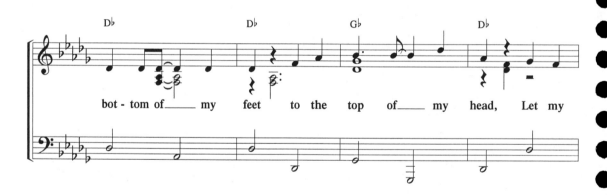

bot - tom of____ my feet to the top of____ my head, Let my

life be one big "Hal - le - lu - jah." From the

Hal - le - lu - jah,____ glo - ry, hal - le-lu.____

Hal - le - lu - jah,____ hal - le, hal - le-lu - jah,____

Hal - le - lu - jah,____ glo - ry, hal - le-lu.____

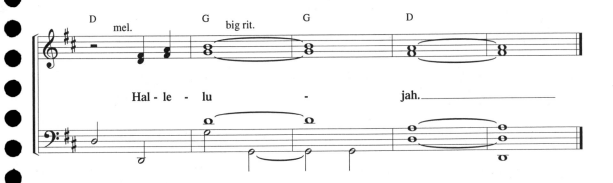

Hal - le - lu - jah.____

Great Big Beautiful World

LINDA REBUCK

TOM FETTKE

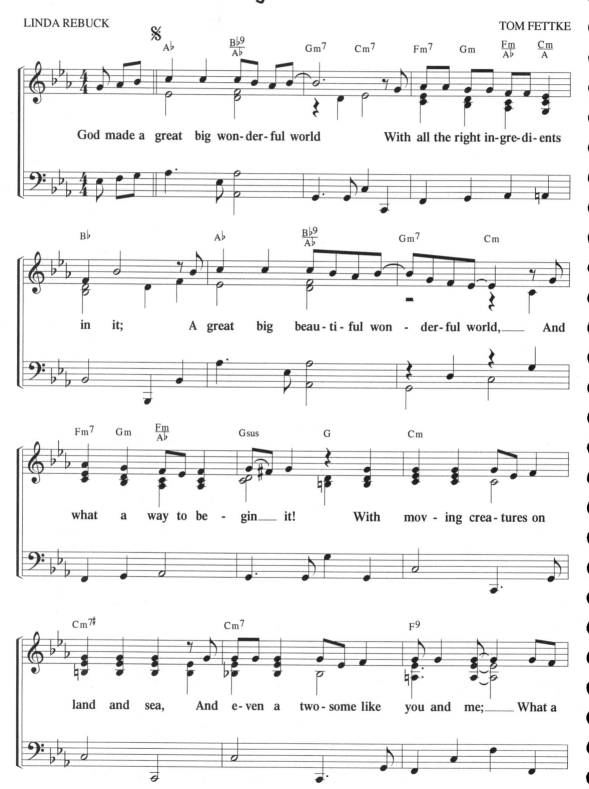

God made a great big won-der-ful world With all the right in-gre-di-ents in it; A great big beau-ti-ful won-der-ful world,___ And what a way to be - gin___ it! With mov-ing crea-tures on land and sea, And e-ven a two-some like you and me;___ What a

Jesus Loves

Anonymous

JILL FREEMAN
Arr. by Joseph Linn

black and white; Red, yel - low, black and white; Red,

loves the lit - tle chil - dren, All__ the

yel - low, black and white; Red, yel - low, black and white;

chil - dren of the world.___

Red, yel - low, black and white;_____ They are pre - cious in His

Red, yel - low, black and white;_____ They are pre - cious in His

sight.___ Je - sus loves, Je - sus

sight.___ Je - sus loves, Je - sus

loves, Red, yel - low, black and white;

loves the chil - dren of the world.___

Red, yel - low, black and white.

ABUNDAWONDERFUL MEDLEY

"I Heard About" both verses, medley ending 2nd time. "'Abundawonderful' Life in Jesus" both verses, medley ending 2nd time.

183
I Heard About

Words and Music by
RALPH CARMICHAEL
Arr. by Joseph Linn

li-ons' den. I heard a-bout   lit-tle   Dav-id   pick-in' up   five   smooth
hair   to   grow. I heard a-bout   old___ Jo-nah   learn-in' to   do   God's

stones.
will.   But great-er than all   these   mir-a-cles Is some-thing that hap-pened to

me   the day   that Je-sus   came in-to   my   heart   to   stay.

stay._____   stay.

Je-sus   came   in-to   my   heart   to   stay._____

184 "Abundawonderful" Life in Jesus

Words and Music by
KATHIE HILL
Arr. by Joseph Linn

Eb · Bb · Bb7

liv - ing,
last - ing;
Je - sus gives you joy when you are
Je - sus gives you love when you're a -

Eb · F

sad.
lone.
He gives hope when days are drea - ry,
He gives peace when you are wor - ried,

Bb · F

Strength when you are wear - y;
Pa - tience when you're hur - ried;
He can make life cheer - y, E - ven
When your day is blur - ry, He is

1 Song and medley ending; 2 Song ending · D. S.

Bb · Ab/Bb · Bb/D · Bb · Ab/Bb · Bb7

when things look bad!
still in con - trol!
There is a -

2 Medley ending

Bb · Ab/C · Bb/D · B · A/C# · B/D# · B · A/B · B7

still in con - trol! There is a -

The New 23rd

Adapted from Psalm 23 by RALPH CARMICHAEL

RALPH CARMICHAEL

Be - cause the Lord is my Shep - herd, I have ev - ery-thing_that I

need._____ He lets me rest in mead - ows green And__

leads__ me_____ be - side the qui - et stream. He keeps on giv - ing

life to me And__ helps__ me to do what hon - ors Him the most.

It's a Miracle

WILLIAM J. GAITHER
and GLORIA GAITHER

WILLIAM J. GAITHER

*1. What drives the stars with-out mak-ing a sound? _____
2. Who shows the birds how to make a good nest? _____
*(3.) spring makes a brook and a brook makes a stream, The

Why don't they crash _____ when they're spin-ning a - round?
How can the geese _____ fly so far with-out rest?
stream makes the riv - er wa-ter fresh as can be.

What holds me up when the _____ world's up - side down? I
Why do the ducks _____ go _____ south and not west? I
Who puts the salt in when it gets to the sea? I

know: _____ it's a mir-a-cle. _____ Who tells the
know: _____ it's a mir-a-cle. _____ What makes a
know: _____ it's a mir-a-cle. _____ There are thou-sands of

*Verses 1 and 3 on recording.

LATE ELEMENTARY

He can make a mir-a-cle of me! 3. When a

187 No Mountain High Enough

Words and Music by
CHARLES KIRBY

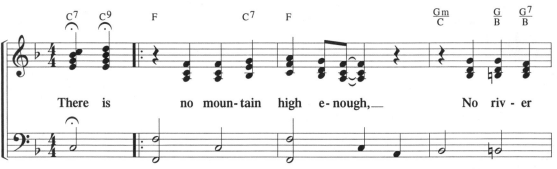

There is no moun-tain high e-nough,— No riv-er

wide e-nough,— No o-cean deep e-nough— To sep-a-rate me from

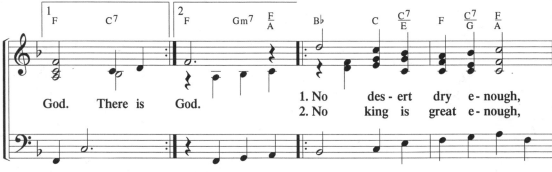

God. There is God. 1. No des-ert dry e-nough,
2. No king is great e-nough,

Gentle Shepherd

GLORIA GAITHER and
WILLIAM J. GAITHER

WILLIAM J. GAITHER
Arr. by Joseph Linn

189 He's Got Everything Under Control

Words and Music by
EDDIE SMITH

*Verses 1, 3-4 on recording.

Soon and Very Soon

Words and Music by
ANDRAÉ CROUCH

*1. Soon and ver - y soon____ we are goin' to see the King.____
*2. No more cry - in' there,____ we are goin' to see the King.____
3. No more dy - in' there,____ we are goin' to see the King.____

Soon and ver - y soon____ we are goin' to see the King.____
No more cry - in' there,____ we are goin' to see the King.____
No more dy - in' there,____ we are goin' to see the King.____

Soon and ver - y soon____ we are goin' to see the King.____
No more cry - in' there,____ we are goin' to see the King.____ Hal - le -
No more dy - in' there,____ we are goin' to see the King.____

lu - jah, hal - le - lu - jah,____ we're goin' to see the King.

____ Hal - le - lu - jah, hal - le -

lu - jah, hal - le - lu - jah!

The Trees of the Field

Adapted from Isaiah 55:12 by STEFFI GEISER RUBIN

STUART DAUERMANN

You shall go out with joy____ and be led forth with peace.____ The moun-tains and the hills will break forth be - fore you. There'll be shouts of joy,____ and all the trees of the

Faith

Words and Music by
FRANK HERNANDEZ and
SHERRY SAUNDERS POWELL

Without faith it's im-pos-si-ble,_____ it's im-pos-si-ble,_____ It's im-pos-si-ble_____ to please God. He who comes to God must be-lieve that He is, And He re-wards those who seek Him. All things are pos-si-ble,_____ all things are pos-si-ble,_____ All things are pos-si-ble;

LATE ELEMENTARY

just be - lieve. God will do ev - ery - thing that He says He will
do, And He re - wards those who seek Him.

193

Who Can Do Anything?

Words and Music by
SALLY GOODWIN
Arr. by Joseph Linn

With a shuffle ♩ = 58

1st time
Unison
1. Who owns the cat - tle on a thou - sand hills, Gives to us and

2nd time
Unison
2. Who makes us hap - py though we've been sad, Loves us e - ven

By Faith

Words and Music by
DAN WHITTEMORE

1. By faith I be-lieve__ God spoke__ worlds in-to__ ex - is - tence, So that all I see was made of things I can-not see. By faith I be-lieve__ God formed the first man in His im-age, Breathed in Him the breath of life, the same He breathed__ in me.

2. By faith I be-lieve__ God lives and cares for His__ cre - a - tion; And though I of - ten fail Him, He will nev - er turn__ a - way. By faith I en-trust__ to Him this life that He has giv - en; And just as saints of old, by faith, His Word I will__ o - bey.

3. If per - chance You're still__ not sure of what I've just__ been say - ing, Please con - sid - er, if you will, the world and all__ you see. God said He re-veals__ Him - self to all through His__ cre - a - tion. O - pen up your heart and by faith sing this song__ with me: I am

not des-cend-ed of mon-keys, though you may be fooled_ at first glance.

I'm the work of God,_ my Cre - a - tor; I am not a prod-uct of

chance. I did not e-volve_ from a tad-pole who got lost and wan-

- dered a - shore; But by God's hand,_ His will, and plan,_ I

1st & 2nd times: D. S.
3rd time: Fine

am_ and noth - ing more.

THE PEACE LOVE JOY MEDLEY

"I've Got Peace Like a River" all verses, medley ending 3rd time. "Down in My Heart" all verses, medley ending 3rd time.

195

I've Got Peace Like a River

Spiritual
Arr. by Joseph Linn

1. I've got peace like a river, I've got peace like a river, I've got
2. I've got love like an ocean, I've got love like an ocean, I've got
3. I've got joy like a fountain, I've got joy like a fountain, I've got

LATE ELEMENTARY

foun - tain, Love like an o - cean, I've got
peace like a riv - er in my soul.

196

Down in My Heart

Words and Music by
GEORGE W. COOKE
Arr. by Joseph Linn

1. I have the
2. I have the
3. I have the

joy, joy, joy, joy down in my heart,
peace that pass - eth un - der - stand - ing down in my heart,
love of Je - sus, love of Je - sus down in my heart,

197

Can You Imagine?

Words and Music by
JANETTE SMART

1. Can you im - ag - ine how it feels to know the God who made the
2. Can you im - ag - ine how it feels to have a Friend who nev - er

earth and sky and sea?
slum - bers, nev - er sleeps?

When He cre - at - ed all the u - ni - verse, His might - y plan in -
Can you be - lieve that when He comes in - to your heart and says He'll

clud - ed you and me.
live there, it's for keeps?

Well, this ex - pe - ri - ence is not im - ag - in - a - tion;

It's a fact, oh yes, it's true.

And I just can't keep it to my - self; I'll

pass it on to you.

you, and you, and you, and you.

If You Believe

Words and Music by
MOSIE LISTER

*1. I read about_____ how Paul and Silas were in jail, And no one
*2. When Daniel sat_____ within the hungry lions' den, Nobody
3. When David stood_____ before the giant with his sling, Goliath

there,_____ nobody there could go their bail. But when they prayed,_____ they found that
thought_____ that there was any hope for him. But all night long,_____ the lions
laughed_____ at such a puny little thing. But David knew_____ his faith in

God was on their side; The jailhouse door_____ swung open wide._____
never took a bite; God took away_____ their appetite._____
God would stand the test. He flung the rock;_____ God did the rest._____

Refrain

If you believe,_____ you shall receive._____ There's not a

*Verses 1 and 2 on recording

trou-ble or care the good Lord can't re-lieve.   O   He is just the same to-day.

All you have to do is just trust and pray and be-lieve,____ you must be-lieve.____

God Takes Good Care of Me

199

Words and Music by
HENRY SLAUGHTER
Arr. by Joseph Linn

Brightly, with a shuffle feel ♩ = 144

1. God   takes____ real good
2. God   takes____ real good

LATE ELEMENTARY: GOD'S LOVE AND CARE

God takes good care of_____ me.

me. God takes good

care of, He real-ly takes good care of me._____ God takes good

care of_____ me. *He real-ly takes good care of me.*
(spoken)

I'm Gonna Hide God's Word Inside My Heart 200

Words and Music by
PETER and HANNEKE JACOBS
Arr. by Joseph Linn

I'm gon - na hide God's Word in - side my heart And

learn each verse from mem - o - ry.

Fill in the Blanks

DOTTIE RAMBO

DOTTIE RAMBO and
DAVE HUNTSINGER
Arr. by Joseph Linn

1. Out in the sea, in the mid-dle of the deep___ blue
2. Up in a tree, in the top___ of a syc-a-more
3. Down in the den, in the bot-tom of the li-ons'

sea, A great___ big___ whale was___ swim-min' by, And
tree, Sat a lit-tle man on a limb so high. He
den, The King___ threw___ *(whoop)* to the hun-gry beasts; The

boy,___ was he in___ for a big sur-prise! He o-pened His mouth, and___
heard___ that___ *(whoop)* would be pass-in' by. He was___ so short that he
li-ons get-tin' read-y for a great big feast. They smacked their mouths and they

Rock on Rock

JANETTE SMART

TERRY CAMSEY

There was a man;— he had a plan___ That he would build him a house, a house that was brand new. So he looked a-round,— found a piece of ground,— And he said to him-self,

(1) "Self,
(2) "The

this-'ll
best will

203

Father Abraham

Traditional
Arr. by Joseph Linn

1. Right arm: move right arm back and forth like walking, with fist clenched and elbow bent.
   Do this motion while singing through the song again.
2. Left arm: add the left arm in the same manner as the right.
3. Right foot: add the right leg stepping up and down.
4. Left foot: add the left foot, so that you are walking in place.
5. Chin up: add chin moving up and down.
6. Turn around: turn in place while doing all of the above.
7. Sit down: the end!

Take Off Those Rags, Lazarus

Words and Music by
BILL CASWELL and
KIM PATTON
Arr. by Joseph Linn

Opt. solo

1. Mar - tha___ and Mar - y,___ they sent for___ the Lord. "Our

broth - er___ is dy - ing!"___ they cried. But Je - sus,___ He lin - gered___ for

Opt. solo & group

Opt. solo

three days___ or more And poor ol' Laz - 'rus, he died.___ "What

2nd time: group

took You___ so long, Lord,___ where have___ You been? It's
2. Just like___ ol' Laz - a - rus, I was___ dead too; I was

too late___ to save him,"___ they said.___ "He's
pay - ing___ the wag - es___ of sin.___ But

205

Adam in the Garden

Caribbean and
SUZANNE H. CLASON

Caribbean

1. Ad-am in the gar-den hid-ing, hid-ing, Hid-ing, hid-ing, hid-ing, hid-ing.
2. When God speaks, I'll be there lis-t'ning, Be there lis-t'ning, be there lis-t'ning.

Ad-am in the gar-den hid-ing, hid-ing, Hid-ing from the Lord.
When God speaks, I'll be there lis-t'ning, Lis-t'ning to the Lord.

Tell me— where is Ad-am Hid-ing, hid-ing, hid-ing, hid-ing?
"Here am I," I'll an-swer, Lis-t'ning, lis-t'ning, lis-t'ning, lis-t'ning.

Tell me— where is Ad-am Hid-ing from the Lord?
"Here am I," I'll an-swer, Lis-t'ning to the Lord.

Volunteers

206

Words and Music by
JOANNE BARRETT and RON E. LONG

Humbly Grateful or Grumbly Hateful?

Words and Music by
KATHIE HILL and JANET MCMAHAN

Are you hum-bl-y grate-ful or grum-bl-y hate-ful? What's your at-ti-tude?___ Do you grum-ble and groan___ or let it be known_ You're grate-ful for all God's done for you?___

1. When Jo-nah found him-self in the
2. When No-ah found him-self in the

THE FRUIT OF THE SPIRIT MEDLEY

"The Fruit of the Spirit" 1 time. "The Fruit Song" verses 1 & 2, medley ending 2nd time.

208

The Fruit of the Spirit

Words and Music by
PETER and HANNEKE JACOBS
Arr. by Joseph Linn

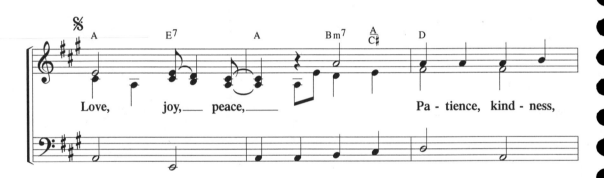

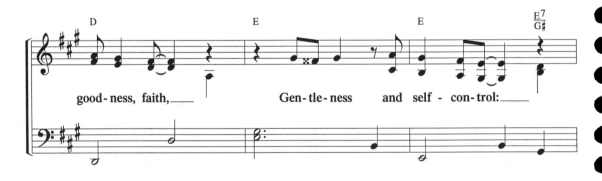

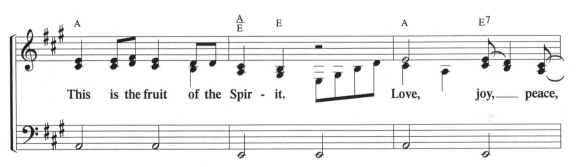

209 The Fruit Song

Words and Music by
JOANNE BARRETT
Arr. by Joseph Linn

God. The fruit of the Spir-it of God.

I'm grow - ing, I'm grow - ing; There's a

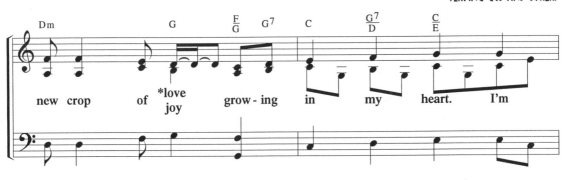

new crop of *love joy grow-ing in my heart. I'm

grow - ing, I'm grow - ing; There's a

Song ending (D. S.)

new crop of *love joy in my heart.

Medley ending Conclusion of medley

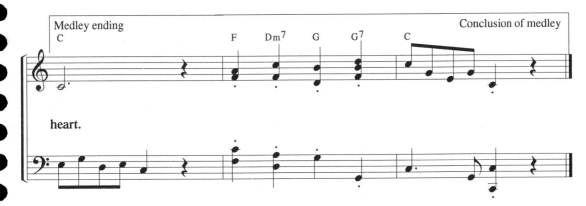

heart.

*Additional verses: peace, patience, kindness, goodness, faith, gentleness, self-control.

God Spoke

Words and Music by
CHARLOTTE GAUS

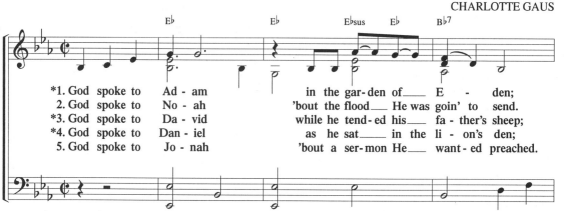

*1. God spoke to Ad - am / in the gar-den of___ E - den;
2. God spoke to No - ah / 'bout the flood___ He was goin' to send.
*3. God spoke to Da - vid / while he tend-ed his___ fa-ther's sheep;
*4. God spoke to Dan - iel / as he sat___ in the li - on's den;
5. God spoke to Jo - nah / 'bout a ser-mon He___ want-ed preached.

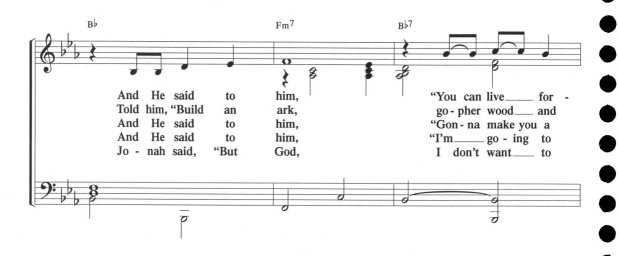

And He said to him, / "You can live___ for -
Told him, "Build an ark, / go - pher wood___ and
And He said to him, / "Gon - na make you a
And He said to him, / "I'm___ go - ing to
Jo - nah said, "But God, / I don't want___ to

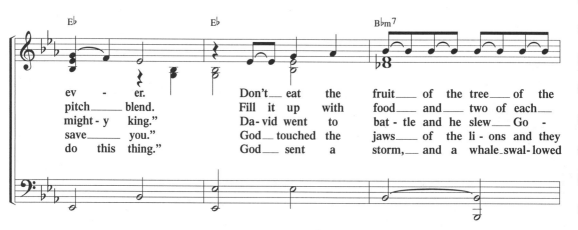

ev - er. / Don't___ eat the / fruit___ of the tree___ of the
pitch___ blend. / Fill it up with / food___ and___ two of each___
might - y king." / Da - vid went to / bat - tle and he slew___ Go -
save___ you." / God___ touched the / jaws___ of the li - ons and they
do this thing." / God___ sent a / storm,___ and a whale swal - lowed

*Verses 1, 3 and 4 on recording.

Eb7 / Ab / Ab

knowl- edge of____ good____ and   e - vil."   But the dev - il said,____
crea - ture that____ roams____ the   earth."_____   No - ah did____ just____
li - ath with a ti - ny   stone;_____   And he wrote____ some____
all____ be - gan____ to   purr._____   So____ Dan - iel was de -
Jo - nah till he said,____ "I'll   go!"_____   So____ he went____ to____

Eb / Ebsus Eb / Bb7 / Eb / Eb

"Do,"____ and he ate____ the____ fruit; Should have lis - tened to the   Lord.
that____ and he lived to tell the tale, 'Cause he lis - tened to the   Lord.
psalms____ and he did____ great____ things 'Cause he lis - tened to the   Lord.
liv - ered and he was - n't a - fraid 'Cause he lis - tened to the   Lord.
Nin - e - veh and preached____ God's____ Word And he lis - tened to the   Lord.

Refrain

Bb / Bb7 / Eb

God spoke to him_____ like He speaks to   all   of   us;_____

Eb / Bb / 1-4 Fm7 / Gm/Bb Bb7

_____ And we'd all be bet - ter   off   if we'd lis - ten to   what He has to

Eb / D.C. Eb / 5 Fm7 / Bb7 / Eb / Eb7/G Ab Eb

say._____   what He has to   say._____

The Family of God

WILLIAM J. GAITHER
and GLORIA GAITHER

WILLIAM J. GAITHER

I'm so glad   I'm a part   of the fam - 'ly of   God—   I've been

washed   in the foun - tain,_____   cleansed by   His blood!

Joint heirs   with Je - sus   as we trav - el   this   sod;   For I'm

part   of the fam - 'ly,_____   the fam - 'ly of   God._____

Saints Society

Words and Music by
HARLAN MOORE
Arr. by Joseph Linn

We're the Saints So - ci - e - ty,_____ Part of God's big fam - i - ly;_____ Kind and for - giv - ing, We're grow - ing and liv - ing in Je - sus ev - ery day._____ We're the Saints So - ci - e - ty,_____ Prais - ing God in un - i - ty;_____ Pray - ing and car - ing And

Zeroes into Heroes

JOANNE BARRETT
and DWIGHT THOMAS

DWIGHT THOMAS
Arr. by Joseph Linn

*1. God can take those ze - roes / And turn them in - to he - roes. / He did it all through his - to - ry;___ He can do it a - gain to - day. / He'll take your fear and doubt - ing / And

2. God can take your trou - bles / And pop them like they're bub - bles. / He did it all through his - to - ry;___ He can do it a - gain to - day. / And when your faith is sag - ging, / He'll

*3. When you feel like noth - ing / And you've lost all your stuff - ing, / Re - mem - ber God is still num - ber one.___ Is He your num - ber one to - day? / For when He stands be - side you / And

*Verses 1 and 3 on recording.

SHOW HIS LOVE MEDLEY

"Heart to Change the World" both verses, coda. "My Hands Are the Hands" all verses, medley ending last time.

214

Heart to Change the World

Words and Music by
DEBBY RETTINO
Arr. by Joseph Linn

1. You and I've_____ got to have_ a heart to change the world._____
2. Je-sus told_____ us to go_ and share in ev-ery land,_____

Let the song_____ start to sing_ in ev-ery boy and girl.
O-ver seas,_____ through the hills,_ a-cross the des-ert sand._____

Start to share,_____ start to care_____ from a heart of love.
By God's grace,_____ in God's strength,_____ we can change the world.

My Hands Are the Hands

Words and Music by
DEBBY RETINO
Arr. by Joseph Linn

1. My hands are the hands that God will use To show the world His love. When people look at me, they'll see A bit of heav'n above.
2. My feet are the feet that God will use To carry forth the light. If people will believe in Him, They can have eternal life.
3. My voice is the voice that God will use To tell the world He cares, To let them know He loves them so— All people everywhere.

O

Jesus Is a Gentleman

Words and Music by
KATHIE HILL
Arr. by Joseph Linn

Je - sus is a gen - tle - man who
Je - sus is a gen - tle - man who

nev - er forc - es His way in. He stands knock - ing
waits so pa - tient - ly and then He prays you will

at your door un - til you let Him in.
ask Him in to

SERVANT MEDLEY

"Servant of All" 1 time. "Make Me a Servant" 2 times.

217

Servant of All

Words and Music by
MICHAEL RYAN

With a shuffle

If you want to be great_____ in God's king - dom,_____ Learn to be the ser - vant of all.

If you want to be great_____ in God's king - dom,_____ Learn to be the ser - vant of

Make Me a Servant

Words and Music by
KELLY WILLARD

Make me a ser-vant, hum-ble and meek; Lord, let me lift up those who are weak. And may the prayer of my heart al-ways be: Make me a ser-vant, make me a ser-vant, Make me a ser-vant to-day.

Conclusion of medley

Search My Heart

219

Words and Music by
TWILA PARIS
Arr. by Joseph Linn

Search my heart, make me clean;
It's Your ap-prov-al__ I long for. Rule my life,
be my King. Do what You will; I__ be-long to
You. You. It's Your ap-
prov-al__ I long for.

rit.

220 I Am Thankful to Be an American

Words and Music by
OTIS SKILLINGS
Arr. by Joseph Linn

March feel ♩ = ca. 120

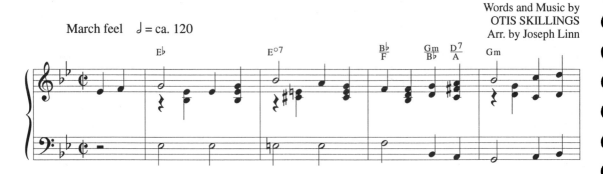

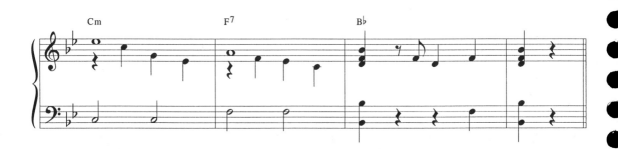

I am thank-ful to be an A - mer - i - can_____ And to

live in the great-est land of all._____ In a

O Come, All Ye Faithful

From the Latin, 18th Century
Tr. by Frederick Oakeley

From Wade's "Cantus Diversi," 18th Century
Arr. by Lyndell Leatherman

1. O come, all ye faith - ful, Joy - ful and tri - um - phant. O come ye, O come___ ye to Beth - le - hem. Come and be - hold Him— Born the King of an - gels.

2. Yea, Lord, we greet Thee, Born this hap - py morn - ing. O Je - sus, to Thee___ be all glo - ry giv'n: Word of the Fa - ther, Now in flesh ap - pear - ing.

O come, let us a - dore Him! O come, let us a - dore Him! O come, let us a - dore Him,___ Christ___ the Lord!

Worship the King

Words and Music by
BILLY SMILEY
and **BILL GEORGE**
Arr. by Joseph Linn

Come, let us wor-ship the King.

Je-sus, the Sav-ior, is born; For the Lord will

reign o - ver all_____ the earth.

Deck the Halls

KEN BIBLE and Traditional

Welsh Melody
Arr. by Joseph Linn

1. Deck the halls with boughs of hol - ly,
2. See the Ho - ly Child be - fore us,

Fa la la la la la la la la. 'Tis the sea - son
Fa la la la la la la la la. Rise and join the

to be jol - ly, Fa la la la la la la la la.
an - gel cho - rus, Fa la la la la la la la la.

Praise to the Infant King

NAN ALLEN

DENNIS ALLEN
Arr. by Joseph Linn

Rejoice!

LINDA REBUCK

DAVID HUNTSINGER
Arr. by Joseph Linn

Joyful, Joyful, We Adore You

LINDA LEE JOHNSON

LUDWIG VAN BEETHOVEN
Arr. by Joseph Linn

1. Joy - ful, joy - ful, we a - dore You, God of glo - ry, Lord of light;
2. All Your works de - clare Your glo - ry; All cre - a - tion joins to sing.

An - gels lift - ing praise be - fore You Sing through - out this ho - ly night.
Praise re - sounds as earth re - joic - es In the birth of Christ, the King.

In a man - ger lies a - ba - by, Child of Mar - y, Son of God.
Shep - herds kneel be - fore the In - fant; Trum - pets sound and an - thems raise,

(D.S.)

Voic - es joined in joy - ful cho - rus Praise You for Your gift of love.
As with joy our hearts are lift - ed, Joined in won - der, love and praise.

Christmas Isn't Christmas
(Till It Happens in Your Heart)

SEASONAL
227

CAROL OWENS

JIMMY and CAROL OWENS
Arr. by Joseph Linn

Christ - mas is - n't Christ - mas till it hap - pens in your heart; Some - where deep in - side you is where Christ - mas real - ly starts. So give your heart to

228   Christ the Lord Is Risen Today

CHARLES WESLEY

From "Lyra Davidica," 1708
Arr. by Joseph Linn

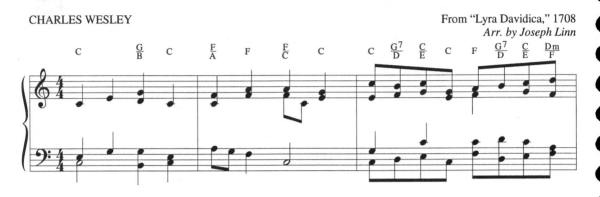

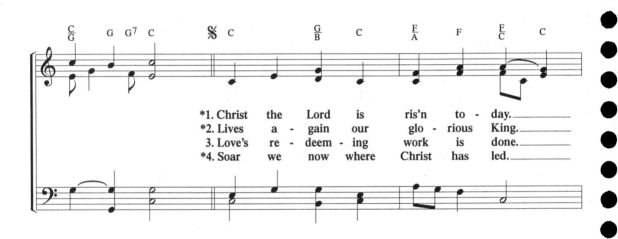

*1. Christ   the   Lord   is   ris'n   to - day.
*2. Lives   a - gain   our   glo - rious   King.
3. Love's   re - deem - ing   work   is   done.
*4. Soar   we   now   where   Christ   has   led.

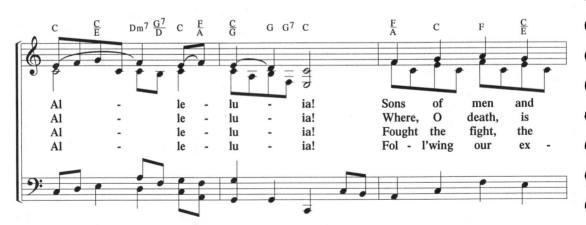

Al - le - lu - ia!   Sons   of   men   and
Al - le - lu - ia!   Where,   O   death,   is
Al - le - lu - ia!   Fought   the   fight,   the
Al - le - lu - ia!   Fol - l'wing   our   ex -

*Verses 1, 2 and 4 on recording.

There Is a Redeemer

Words and Music by
MELODY GREEN
Arr. by Joseph Linn

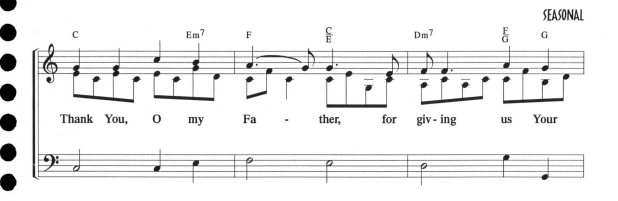

Thank You, O my Fa - ther, for giv - ing us Your

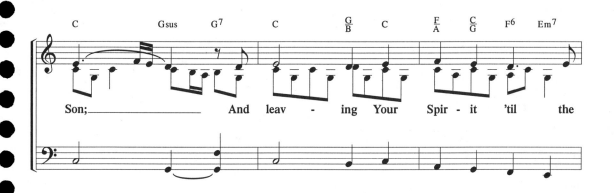

Son;_____ And leav - ing Your Spir - it 'til the

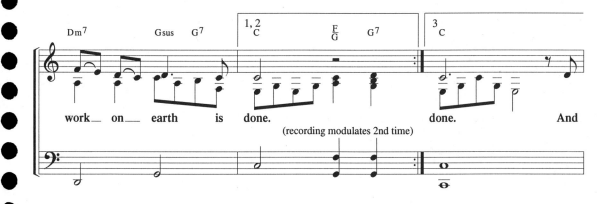

work__ on__ earth is done. done. And

(recording modulates 2nd time)

leav - ing Your Spir - it 'til the work__ on__ earth is done.

230 Jesus Is Alive and Doin' Well

Words and Music by
EDDIE SMITH
Arr. by Joseph Linn

1. I hear
tell that some folks say that God has died, But it
care-ful, ver-y care-ful where you look. You won't

would-n't be the first time some-one lied. He's not
find my Je-sus in some his-t'ry book. He is

ly-ing in some tomb; He's a-live and com-ing soon. I know
not some-one who was, And I tell you this be-cause I know

TOPICAL INDEX

To learn the age-group placement for each song, simply notice the song numbers:

1- 73	Early Childhood
74-153	Early Elementary
154-230	Late Elelmentary

Note, however, that age-group placements in this book are only approximations. Many of these songs are suitable for various age groups.

ACTIVITY/NOVELTY

Arky, Arky	120
Clap Your Hands	1
Exercise Song	47
Father Abraham	203
Fill in the Blanks	201
Get in the Ark!	116
Hallelujah!	82
Hands on Shoulders	42
Head and Shoulders, Knees and Toes	48
Hinges	41
I am a "C"	101
If You Can Sing a Song	89
If You're Happy	2
Let's All Sing Together	3
Only a Boy Named David	112
Open, Shut Them	45
Say to the Lord, I Love You	75
Take Off Those Rags, Lazarus	204
The Wiggle Song	43
Zaccheus	34

BIBLE SONGS

A Happy Home	38
A-B-C-D-E-F-G	106
Actions Speak Louder than Words	140
Adam, Adam	113
Adam in the Garden	205
Arky, Arky	120
Father Abraham	203
Fill in the Blanks	201
Fishers of Men	131
Friends of God	39
Get in the Ark!	116
God Spoke	210
He's Got Everything Under Control	189
Hey, Jonah!	122
Humbly Grateful or Grumbly Hateful?	207
I Heard About	183
I Open My Bible and Read	36
I Wonder How It Felt	137
I'm Gonna Hide God's Word Inside My Heart	200
If You Believe	198
Jesus Is Living in Heaven Today	117
Jesus Loves Even Me	126
John 3:16	121
Let the Children Come to Me	40
Noah	37
Nobody Else	165
Only a Boy Named David	112
Peter, James, and John in a Sailboat	115
Rock on Rock	202
Sandy Land	129

Shadrach, Meshach, and Abednego	114
Take Off Those Rags, Lazarus	204
The B-I-B-L-E	119
The Bible Tells Us Jesus Grew	35
The New 23rd	185
The Wise Man and the Foolish Man	118
There Were Twelve Disciples	111
Zaccheus	34

CHURCH

Everybody Ought to Love Jesus	88
Saints Society	212
Sh-h-h-h	7
The Family of God	211
This Is God's House	10
We Go to Church	12
When to Church I Go	13

CREATION

A Great Big God	110
All Creatures of Our God and King	163
All Things Bright and Beautiful	23
By Faith	194
Can You Imagine?	197
Creature Praise	76
Everything That Is, Is His	98
God Gave Me Eyes	21
God Made Everything	19
God Made Our Wonderful World	17
God's Care	18
God's Night Light	25
Great Big Beautiful World	181
Great Is Thy Faithfulness	174
He's Got the Whole World in His Hands	100
Hinges	41
I Often Think of God	24
I'm Something Special	128
If I Were the Wind	20
It's a Miracle	186
Joyful, Joyful, We Adore Thee	164
Kids Under Construction	124
My God Is So Big	97
Nighttime Thoughts	26
Nobody Else	165
The Butterfly Song	127
We Were Made to Love the Lord	74
What a Wonderful World	22
Who Can Do Anything?	193
Wonder Song	28
Wonderfully Made	46

CHRISTMAS

Amen!	148
Away in a Manger	71

ALPHABETICAL INDEX

Song and *Medley* Titles